Contents

The Law and Tradition as they affect Walking in Scotland; Scotland's Hills and Mountains: a Concordat on Access; Glossary of Gaelic Names; Safety on the Hills; Useful Organisations; Ordnance Survey Maps; Bibliography

Short, easy walks

Walks of modest length, likely to involve some modest uphill walking

More challenging walks which may be longer and/or over more rugged terrain, often with some stiff climbs

Keymap

SCALE 1:312 500 or 1 INCH to 5 MILES *1CM to 3.1 KM*

KILOMETRES

MILES

KEYMAP HEIGHTS SHOWN IN FEET

pathfinder guide

Fort William *and* Glen Coe

WALKS

Compiled by
Hamish Brown
and Neil Wilson

ARROLD

Ordnance
Survey

Acknowledgements

I would like to thank many people, including the Forestry
Commission Area Planning Officer, the staff at Fort William
and Spean Bridge tourist information offices, many keepers
and local contacts (to whom this is home territory) and friends
who walked many of the routes. All these I am sure helped to
make the book more worthy of the splendid area it portrays.

Text:	Hamish Brown, Neil Wilson
Photography:	Hamish Brown, Jarrold Publishing, Neil Wilson
Editors:	Thomas Albrighton, Donald Greig, Geoffrey Sutton
Designers:	Brian Skinner, Doug Whitworth
Mapping:	Heather Pearson, Sandy Sims
Series Consultant:	Brian Conduit

Jarrold Publishing   ISBN 0-7117-0571-2

While every care has been taken to ensure the accuracy of the
route directions, the publishers cannot accept responsibility
for errors or omissions, or for changes in details given. The
countryside is not static: hedges and fences can be removed,
field boundaries can alter, footpaths can be rerouted and
changes in ownership can result in the closure or diversion of
some concessionary paths. Also, paths that are easy and
pleasant for walking in fine conditions may become slippery,
muddy and difficult in wet weather, while stepping-stones
across rivers and streams may become impassable.

If you find an inaccuracy in the text or maps, please write
to Jarrold Publishing or Ordnance Survey respectively at one
of the addresses below.

First published 1992
by Jarrold Publishing and Ordnance Survey
Reprinted 1994, 1996, 1998

Printed in Great Britain
by Jarrold Book Printing, Thetford, Norfolk 4/98

Jarrold Publishing
Whitefriars, Norwich NR3 1TR
Ordnance Survey
Romsey Road, Southampton SO16 4GU

Front cover: Loch Leven, near Kinlochleven
Previous page: The mountains of Glen Coe from Loch Linnhe

Keymap

At-a-glance...

Walk	Page	Start	Distance	Time	Highest Point
Arkaig Glens	40	Eas Chia-aig (waterfall)	7 miles (11.25km)	3½ hrs	1444ft (440m)
A Ballachulish Walk	56	Ballachulish	7 miles (11.25km)	3½ hrs	1312ft (400m)
Beinn Dorain	74	Bridge of Orchy	5½ miles (8.75km)	4½ hrs	3524ft (1074m)
Beinn Teallach	72	Roughburn	9 miles (14.5km)	4½ hrs	3003ft (915m)
Ben Nevis	87	Glen Nevis Youth Hostel, or Achintee	8 miles (12.75km)	6–7 hrs	4418ft (1344m)
Ben Starav	84	Coileitir road-end, Glen Etive	7½ miles (12km)	5½–6 hrs	3541ft (1078m)
Ben Tee	76	Laggan Locks	8½ miles (13.5km)	5 hrs	2957ft (901m)
Blackrock and Bà Bridge	28	Blackrock, Rannoch Moor	6 miles (9.5km)	3 hrs	1673ft (510m)
Caledonian Canal	34	Gairlochy	8 miles (12.75km)	3½ hrs	164ft (50m)
Cameron Country	46	East end of Loch Arkaig	7 miles (11.25km)	3½ hrs	164ft (50m)
Fraoch Bheinn	64	West end of Loch Arkaig	4½ miles (7.25km)	3½ hrs	2815ft (858m)
Glen Roy – The Parallel Roads	38	Brae Roy Lodge	8½ miles (13.5km)	3½ hrs	984ft (300m)
Gondola Walks, Nevis Range	34	Nevis Range gondola station	6 miles (9.5km)	4 hrs	2175ft (663m)
Hospital Lochan, Glencoe	18	Glencoe village	3 miles (4.75km)	2 hrs	180ft (55m)
Inchree Waterfalls	16	Inchree, near Corran Ferry	3 miles (4.75km)	2 hrs	262ft (80m)
The Heights of Kinlochleven	69	Kinlochleven	10 miles (16km)	5½ hrs	1312ft (400m)
Leum Uilleim	62	Corrour Station	8 miles (12.75km)	4 hrs	2972ft (906m)
Loch Etive Shore Walk	31	Foot of Glen Etive	6 miles (9.5km)	3 hrs	886ft (270m)
Round Loch Ossian	51	Corrour Station	9 miles (14.5km)	4½ hrs	1345ft (410m)
Secretive Loch Treig	66	Corrour Station	9 miles (14.5km)	4½ hrs	1329ft (405m)
Mamore Lodge	24	Kinlochleven	3½ miles (5.5km)	2½ hrs	846ft (258m)
Nevis Gorge and Steall Falls	26	Head of Glen Nevis road	3 miles (4.75km)	2½ hrs	820ft (250m)
Pap of Glencoe	54	Glencoe village	5 miles (8km)	3½ hrs	2434ft (742m)
On to Rannoch Moor	43	Rannoch Station	8 miles (12.75km)	4 hrs	1148ft (350m)
The Stalker's Path on Beinn na Caillich	48	Kinlochleven	7½ miles (12km)	4½ hrs	2607ft (764m)
Stob Ban	82	Polldubh, Glen Nevis	6½ miles (10.5km)	5½ hrs	3274ft (999m)
Stob Ghabhar	79	Victoria Bridge	9½ miles (15.25km)	6 hrs	3566ft (1087m)
The Two Passes	59	Upper Glen Coe	9 miles (14.5km)	4½ hrs	1640ft (500m)

Comments

This walk starts and finishes by a dainty waterfall and circles Glas Bheinn (2402ft/732m), bridging the contrast between wooded and barren glens and covering some fine loch views.

Ballachulish, once a slate-mining village, nestles by the shores of Loch Leven. The area offers this walk up into the hills behind, along an old pre-road route to Appin and Benderloch.

From the A82 from Tyndrum this shapely cone-shaped hill bursts dramatically into view, a challenge to every walker and best ascended from Bridge of Orchy, as in this walk.

Up by the valley and down again by a ridge gives the walker plenty of variety in the ascent of this hill which was only recently designated a Munro. The view to Loch Treig is fine.

Britain's highest summit is a popular ascent – the cliff-edge summit has a majestic 360˚ panorama – but even the 'tourist route' is a demanding and serious venture. Reserve it for settled weather.

A big granite peak of character with a fine seaward setting above Loch Etive, at the end of a remote road approach. A long ascent from sea level which should not be taken lightly.

Instantly recognisable, Corbett Ben Tee loses nothing to its neighbouring Munros and gives a classic walk by canal locks and a wide loch, through glen, falls and moorland, to the summit panorama.

The name 'Rannoch Moor' has a certain aura about it. This walk skirts the western edge of the moor on historic tracks and offers wide panoramic views, so keep it for a clear day.

Telford's greatest engineering feat offers almost level walking so one can breathe in the atmosphere of the Great Glen and distant Ben Nevis. Walk early or late to avoid traffic risks.

Loch Arkaig lies west of the great Glen and is romantically associated with the clan Cameron. Take a picnic and make it a day out, visiting Achnacarry Castle.

Remote and 2815ft (858m) high, this craggy Corbett lies at the end of the winding but beautiful drive west along Loch Arkaig. A real mountain in a wilderness setting.

The Parallel Roads are a freak of nature, seen all the way up Glen Roy. The enjoyably remote walk continues beyond to take in a fine waterfall, the Eas Ban.

Scotland's only mountain gondola (convenient for Fort William) gives easy access and is an experience in itself. The views over Lochaber and up the Great Glen are magnificent.

A hidden gem of a walk in lush woodlands to contrast with the stark hills and grim history of Glen Coe. May–June sees the rhododendrons in flower, charmingly reflected in the quiet waters of a sunny day.

A walk of remarkably easy access (just off the A82), taking in a charming series of falls, best in spring or autumn when the trees are colourful and the water plentiful.

A longish and strenuous round which nonetheless offers varied and spectacular scenery, deserving of a full day. A shorter version is possible.

The starting point is quite high up, so the ascent of this peak is made easier. Well worth a clear day for the view along Loch Ossian and to wild hill country to the west, but avoid the stalking season.

A twisty road leads down Glen Etive to end by this sea loch, the shores of which offer a rough tranquillity as well as views of Cruachan, Ben Starav and other big mountains.

A good walk from the West Highland Line (Corrour Station) along an estate road, making a circuit round charming Loch Ossian, set among high hills.

'The Road to the Isles' was once a cattle-droving route, and this walk follows part of it at the south end of Loch Treig, reached from remote Corrour Station.

This walk lifts the pedestrian high to enhance the experience of forest, hill and fjord, and uses part of an old military road, now the West Highland Way.

At the head of Glen Nevis, this walk goes through a gorge of Himalayan character to come on a meadowland backed by one of the most lovely 'bridal veil' falls, the An Steall Ban.

A landmark hill easily seen from all round the Ballachulish area, the Pap is a superlative viewpoint in itself once climbed, the view being ample reward for 2434ft (742m) of hard ascent.

The magnificent isolation of the moor lies at the end of this woodland walk west from Rannoch Station, itself full of character (and boasting a platform café).

The steep climb to the summit is eased by a fine stalker's path, and the short-cropped turf of the ridge beyond offers delightful walking with panoramic views of the hills.

One of the finest big peaks of the Mamore range, a path gives reasonable access but the final climb is rough, and some prior experience of Munros is advisable. Avoid the stalking season.

This is a serious mountain walk which gives a fine example of what a bigger Highland hill offers in scale, complexity, variety and setting. This route is best kept for a clear day.

This is a classic walk at the head of Glen Coe, circling the Buachaille Etive Beag ('the small shepherd of Etive') by two historic passes, formed into 'U' shapes by the movements of glaciers.

At-a-glance...

Introduction to
Fort William and Glen Coe

'Scotland is different' is a regular comment of southern visitors. Understanding, and relishing, the differences is part of the fun of exploring the Highlands. There is no walk in this book which could be mistaken for the South Downs, or Cannock Chase, or the Lake District.

Fort William is one of the busiest tourist centres in Scotland and, with Glen Coe to the south, must absorb a high percentage of visiting walkers. This is not surprising as it encompasses one of the great areas of sea and mountain landscape in the country, backed by some of the biggest and most demanding peaks. Small is often even more beautiful, and this guide seeks to give a selection of walks of all grades, and to reward all interests.

The area covered by this guide is roughly that of the local authority Lochaber District, an enlargement of the historical area known as Lochaber. History is much in evidence and its stories are well told at local museums and information centres – Spean Bridge, Fort William, Ballachulish, Kinlochleven, Glencoe – names which ring with historical associations.

The walks in this book have a character of their own within the Scottish context, making them quite different from walks in areas such as the Perthshire hills, the Borders, the Cairngorms or the north-west Highlands. This is Scotland's fjord land, a drowned coastland with long sea arms wending far inland. Roads came only in the 18th century, Caulfeild being one of two great names (he succeeded General Wade, who had constructed the first military roads before the Forty-Five rebellion), Thomas Telford the other; the latter also engineered the Caledonian Canal.

The walks range, uniquely, from sea-level to the highest summit in Britain, so offer a fascinating variety in terms of length, style, and demands on stamina and skill, and this variety makes a word of warning appropriate. Fort William lies at sea-level, on one of the fjords, while a few miles away soars the rugged summit of Ben Nevis, at 4418ft (1344m) the highest point in Britain. People may be ambling along by the former in shirt-sleeves, enjoying the sun, while on the latter a frozen fog rimes the walker in a grey fur as he listens to the Arctic call of a snow-bunting. The variety has its challenging aspect, but how much less rewarding Ben Nevis would be if it were too tame. Most dangers are avoided by using common sense, and pleasures and rewards are all the greater for a certain challenge.

Variations, of course, occur horizontally as well as vertically, and there is great contrast between the first two walks, in woodland settings, and Walk 20 which offers a lonely tramp through utter untamed wilderness. Rannoch Moor, in the heart of the region covered here, could happily swallow the area of the Lake District and much of it lies at 1000ft (300m).

The Lake District is often described as being the Highlands on a smaller scale. For those already familiar with this series of guides the corollary should perhaps be emphasised. In the Highlands the scale is hugely increased and the walks, even middle-grade ones, are thus more demanding, more at the mercy of erratic weather, and often in an unpeopled landscape where commitment and practical skills become even more important. In the Lake District you cannot stray more than a couple of hours away from a road, farm or hamlet; on Rannoch Moor you could walk all day and meet no road, no buildings, no other people.

A practical knowledge of navigating is essential for the walks in the more difficult sections of this book. England has eight 3000-footers, this area around forty, and Ben Nevis and Glen Coe offer more cliffs for climbing than the whole of Lakeland. If it seems this message is being rather hammered home, there is good reason. Ben Nevis and Glen Coe produce a sadly high proportion of the toll of mountain fatalities in Scotland, many of them walkers going unprepared, ill-equipped and inexperienced into this bigger, ambushing world. So, as they say in Scotland, 'Ca' canny'.

Carefulness need not be stultifying, however, and there are plenty of challenging walks in this guide. Too many walkers rest content with a low level of achievement, keeping to 'safe' expeditions, never learning to make decisions, and unable to use map and compass properly.

Garrons (Highland ponies) at Inver Mallie

They have their reward but, in an area such as this, so much of the richness will never be discovered unless there is some striving after greater things. Match prudence with adventurousness, and, as a Napoleonic general taught, 'Every bold advance is to be made with a safe retreat in reserve'.

Another contrast with the Lake District is all too obvious. In Lakeland you are always looking down on a trim, well-populated, cultivated landscape covered with woodlands and farms. In Lochaber, which is both romantic and beautiful, much of the landscape is worn-out, over-exploited, wet desert, the people cleared from it, the inheritance neglected. Rannoch Moor may have a stark beauty but it is a tearful beauty, set in the harsh history of a failed ecology. In the middle of that sea of peat bogs you still come upon magical green swards, with a pile of stones indicative of earlier habitation, and everywhere the flared skeletons of pine roots, pointing out that this wasteland was once a forest. The beauty still smiles – but its history includes periods of dreadful abuse.

Huge forces created this landscape. Ben Nevis and Glen Coe are centres of ancient volcanic activity; their hard rocks (so good for climbing) are the exposed plugs of volcanoes, from which thousands of feet of softer rock have been eroded. Loch Linnhe and the Great Glen are a huge tear fault and geologists have matched places on each side of the tear – now 40 miles (64km) apart. In comparatively recent times glaciers scoured the landscape, biting back into the hills to produce high corries (often holding lochans, small lakes), narrow crests, deep-cut glens and moraine wastelands.

Following the Ice Ages, Scotland became a forested fastness, inhabited by bears, wolves, elk, beavers and other animals which man has now destroyed along with the natural forest itself. And how ugly are most of the modern commercial plantings of alien conifers compared with the remnants one can still see of the natural mix of oak, birch, hazel, Scots pine, aspen, holly and the like. Forests were destroyed to produce agricultural land, for building ships, for smelting, for 'safety', till virtually nothing remained. Lochaber has some remnants of the old forest of Caledon and many of the walks are graced by well-planted woodlands. Woods and water, after all, are vital components of landscape quality.

With the breakdown of the clan system, completed by the horrors of the Forty-Five Jacobite rising, the population expanded and mass emigrations occurred, with a brutal escalation as clan chiefs turned themselves into landowners and cleared whole areas of people to introduce sheep for profit. In Victorian times, the establishment of deer forest for stalking largely completed the process of depopulation. None of this was good for the land, which has simply degenerated into a sour desert. Glen Coe at the time of the massacre (1692) had a population of 140; now there is one small farm.

Fort William occupies an important crossroads. Even in ancient times kings were brought here and shipped to Iona for burial, hence the name Corpach, 'place of corpses'. Traffic plied up and down the Great Glen, or west by Glenfinnan to the sea, or east by Brae Lochaber and Roybridge to the Spey. Glen Coe lay to the south. Here were the clan lands of Camerons, Macdonalds, Stewarts and others, mostly loyal to the Stewart kings. A government fort soon replaced a clan castle and Fort William (300 years old in 1991) has been the centre of the area ever since. Today it is the biggest town in the Highlands between Oban and Inverness, a bit of a hotch-potch, functional rather than attractive, a crossroads, market town, industrial centre – and a vital tourist base for exploring the whole area.

Fort William has an excellent tourist information office, there is the attractive West Highland Museum, and of course books and maps are available through local retail outlets. Reading about the background to an area is part of its enjoyment, and a bibliography in this guide lists selected titles. One or two classic novels with Lochaber settings have also been

Looking over Rannoch Moor from Rannoch Station

mentioned. In view of the area's climate, books can also be a useful 'wet-weather alternative' when a cosy nook in a guest-house may be a greater pleasure than going out in the wind and rain.

One point of similarity with the Lake District is the weather. The rainfall in the Fort William area can be high, up to 120 inches (300cm) a year. This can seriously affect the walks, especially the more demanding ones, where rain and cloud simply lead to slippery conditions, difficult navigation, the risk of exposure, and no views or enjoyment – the very reasons for being there. On such days the historic sites, museums, gardens, reading and easy walks are happier alternatives. Wet weather makes the waterfalls really dramatic spectacles, and both hydro and aluminium works are dependent on a plentiful water supply.

Cloying mist and damp are perfect conditions for the plague of the Highlands, the midge (*Culicoides impunctatus*), which may be a tiny insect, but is always present in vast clouds, friendly as man-eaters. Midges do not like strong sunshine or strong winds and are less active on top of the hills.

Note the use of the word 'hill'. Scotland has its own traditions and terminology and, traditionally, even Ben Nevis is called a hill, the word 'mountain' being an English intrusion. The names of the hills, of glens and burns are largely of Gaelic origin and can look intimidating. *Glen* itself (a narrow valley) is a Gaelic word (*burn* is Lowland Scots). A glossary has been included on page 92 giving the derivation of the commoner elements in the names. *Dubh Lochan* is then seen to be 'black' or 'dark pool', which may be very apt, or *Fraoch Choire,* translated as 'heathery hollow', may be a hint to skirt round to avoid difficult walking. Deciphering this sort of linguistic information can be great fun.

Nobody can walk in Scotland without hearing the terms 'Munro' and 'Corbett'. A Munro is simply a separate hill over 3000ft (914 m) in height, named after the Victorian gentleman who first listed them 100 years ago. People were astonished to find there were 277 such hills in Scotland. Climbing them all is one of the games walkers play, along with climbing the eponymous Corbetts, the listed hills over 2500ft (762m), of which there are 223. Several Munros and Corbetts are the objectives of walks in this book and the term gives a useful shorthand idea of status. Most Corbetts, in their demands, will be the equivalent of the bigger hills of Lakeland or Wales; most Lochaber Munros will present harder challenges than are met south of the border.

Walking and climbing, as popular pastimes, are a fairly recent development, having been taken up by the affluent middle classes last century as a more manly activity than simply following the hordes of tourists captivated by the romanticism of Sir Walter Scott. In the Depression years the unemployed found a welcome escape from the grim towns by heading for the hills, often surviving in (and relishing) the most primitive conditions. The youth hostel movement was born then too. Since the war there has been a steady growth of all mountain pursuits at all levels. The formation of National Parks in England and Wales was indicative of the growing numbers of visitors. Scotland, with its huge area and small population, has not (in the past) felt the need

A view of the Sisters, Glen Coe

for National Parks nor has it faced the problems of access that England has. (The situation, in legal and practical terms, is described on pages 90–92.)

Sadly more Highland estates are being fragmented or bought up by outsiders unfamiliar with both law and tradition; there has also been a huge growth in the number of outdoor enthusiasts, including walkers, likewise often unaware of traditions. The pressure is putting a strain on the fabric of the landscape and the status quo may change. Moves to see National Parks introduced are symptomatic of this. The Scottish Landowners' Federation and the Mountaineering Council of Scotland are increasingly in contact to maintain good relations (see page 91).

Deerstalking is an emotive topic and its main reason often overlooked. Deer are basically forest animals and with the destruction of their habitat they are now having to live in very hard, unnatural conditions. They often have to be fed and numbers controlled by culling, otherwise they starve to death because overgrazing has so impoverished their land. Nobody has devised a better control system than simply shooting the weaker animals.

Unfortunately, many estates under-cull and in a wet, late springtime you may well come upon the sad spectacle of dead deer. The culling of the stags, from mid-August to the end of the third week in October, is a vital part of an estate's economy (and keeping a viable local population going), so at this time walkers are requested to keep off areas being stalked. Obviously this only affects certain places on certain days, and a telephone call or asking locally can usually ensure that nobody's sport is spoilt and no walker risks unnecessary danger. Blanket prohibitions, everywhere and for months on end, are in nobody's interest.

The hinds (females) are culled by the keepers over the winter when there are fewer people on the hills, but the same courtesy is expected; if a Land Rover is seen at a corrie mouth, for instance, it would be very selfish of the walker to barge in and ruin a day's work. Calving time is June and a dappled calf found on a hillside should *not* be touched. It is not abandoned and the returning hind may reject her calf if it smells of humans.

You may be lucky and spot red deer on the open country such as Rannoch Moor or on the higher hills, but they are elusive and timid animals and, in summer, move up a long way to escape midges and heat. In woods you may see the smaller and even more shy roe deer with their eery barks echoing in the woods. Of course, noisy walkers will not see anything.

Early summer rewards with the sight and sound of plentiful wildlife. Rarities like greenshanks and divers are not uncommon on the moors and lochans, eagles can be spotted circling overhead, or a fox glimpsed. In the autumn, the roaring of the stags can be a marvellously evocative sound. The life of pond, river and sea can be interesting and the flowers can excite expert and non-expert alike, from woods full of bluebells (wild hyacinths in Scotland – the 'Scots bluebell' is the harebell) and banks of primroses to delicate alpine rarities. Isolated islets or gorges are often a jungle of trees and flowers as deer and sheep cannot graze in them. Most walkers would enjoy taking binoculars along, as well as a camera.

Even though the landscape looks untouched it is all used one way or another. Cattle are still raised and of course there are sheep – which delight in jumping out in front of nervous car-drivers. The lambing season is April–May, and dogs are best left at home then and routes chosen which will avoid sheep. Dogs are an emotive topic but there is really no need, ever, to have dogs out of control, which simply points to badly trained owners. Routes where sheep farming takes place are indicated.

The National Trust for Scotland was founded in 1931 with the same objectives as its counterpart in England and Wales. Through the years it acquired several mountain areas (Kintail, Torridon, Lawers, Grey Mare's Tail) largely through the benevolence of Percy Unna, a keen walker and

Introduction

climber. Glen Coe was purchased in 1935. For walkers, National Trust for Scotland land offers open access; however, much of Glen Coe is too demanding (or too overcrowded) for the purposes of this guide, but Walk 17 lies on NTS ground.

The Forestry Commission actively encourages walkers in many of its forests (Walks 1, 2, 3, 10, 11, 12, 14 are partly or entirely forest walks), while many other areas (such as in Walk 28) are so heavily used by walkers that no attempt is made to use the hills for other purposes.

It has been hard to select walks for this guide. Many of the Lochaber peaks or ranges are particularly big or demanding (as are Walks 21–28); some areas are less interesting, others are too remote, or access is difficult, or the visitor made unwelcome. But this selection hints at an abundance and it is hoped that the reader will discover plenty more.

The area is dominated by the A82 from the south. This comes over the gateway pass at Tyndrum to Bridge of Orchy (Walk 23), and boldly tackles the Black Mount to cross Rannoch Moor (6) to spectacular Glen Coe (2, 15, 17). Taking the bridge over Loch Leven (1) or driving round by Kinlochleven (4, 13, 21) leads to cheery Fort William, dominated by Ben Nevis (28) and its scenic glen (5, 26). The Great Glen (Glen Albyn) takes the A82 northwards (3, 8), by Loch Lochy (24), to Loch Ness, while west lies lonely Loch Arkaig, offering a variety of walks (10, 12, 19). The A828 from Oban runs up Loch Linnhe through Appin, a fine contrast to the A82 and Rannoch Moor. West of Loch Linnhe one looks to Ardgour, a land of ragged hills and glens. East of the A82 lies one of the largest tracts of virtually uninhabited country in Britain, with – astonishingly – no public roads for access. There is the West Highland Railway Line, however, and this allows some good walks, from Corrour (14, 18, 20) and Rannoch (11) stations. The road west to Mallaig heads out of our area but the road east via Spean Bridge and Roybridge (Brae Lochaber) for Strathspey offers another scenic area (22), including the Parallel Roads in Glen Roy (9).

Several of the more demanding walks can be shortened and still make interesting expeditions. The main variant opportunities are noted in the walks, but one can also walk any distance out and back on the routes.

Few areas in Britain are so well endowed with impressive waterfalls and these walks, not surprisingly, include many of them. Even if full walks are not followed, because of rainy conditions, waterfalls are then at their best and can become alluring objectives for otherwise inclement days. The most noteworthy falls in the walks list are: An Steall Ban (Walk 5), Kilfinnan (24), Inchree (1), the Grey Mare's Fall (4, 21), the Eas Chia-aig (10, 12, 19), and the Eas Ban (9). Also of interest are the Lower Falls of Nevis (5, 26), the Study, Glen Coe (17), and the Robbers' Waterfall on Ben Starav (27).

How rich the area is may be seen from what is *not* covered, often because too demanding: peaks like Bidean nam Bian, the highest in Argyll, which dominates Glen Coe and faces the famous Aonach Eagach ridge, or, at the head of the glen, the rock triangle of the Buachaille Etive Mór. Stob Ghabhar (Walk 25) and Starav (27) are just single peaks in big hill-clusters. The Ben Vair Horseshoe above Ballachulish is left out (although Walk 16 is dominated by it). Walk 26 has only nibbled at the Mamores (a run of twelve Munros), and there is nothing of the Grey Corries, or the Aonachs, or Carn Mor Dearg – ranges with three more peaks over 4000ft (1200m).

It is important to be adequately clothed and shod for Highland walking. The top station of the Gondola (Walk 3) can be much colder, and windier, than the bottom station. A wind- and waterproof jacket should be carried at all times. Good footwear is equally important. Shoes are rarely suitable, even for the easier walks (the path of Walk 5 is one of the roughest, Walk 7 one of the wettest). Lightweight boots are comfortable for normal, dry conditions but for wet conditions mini-wellies are a better option.

The appropriate maps should be carried as a complement to this guide (see page 94), especially for the more demanding walks, where a compass is also essential. Confidence in using map and compass could be a life-saver – and is also good fun. There are no opportunities for refreshments on many of the walks so carry adequate food and drink. Where refreshments are available, usually at the end of a walk, this is mentioned.

The approximate times given refer to the actual walking. To this will have to be added any time spent in halts, picnics, looking at sites, swims and other such activities. If there are museums, visitor centres or sites of interest near a route these are also noted (for instance, Kinlochleven may be industrial but the story of its aluminium production is fascinating and can be learnt at the visitor centre).

Throughout, the word 'path' is used for routes which are primarily for pedestrians only (such as a stalking-path); the word 'track' refers to any rough, unsurfaced way which is usable by forest or estate vehicles (not public cars). 'Road' means a surfaced public motor-road which, in the Highlands, can be a 'narrow road with passing places'. Popular human usage has now effectively created paths up many of the hills described, but relying on these is not a substitute for being able to use map and compass.

When it comes to climbing hills to their summits do take an unhurried approach and a regular rhythm. The hill will not run away, but your energy might if you rush at the ascent (you should be able to talk without gasping!). Keep a gentle angle of attack, too, putting in plenty of zigzags if necessary, just as a road would do on a steep hill.

You can wander round many parts of Britain simply following marked paths, signposts, or other people – with everything made easy, in fact. The Highland landscape is not like that and the walker has to be more self-reliant and prepared to bear the consequence of his own decision-making. This book is only a *guide,* after all. The challenges, the action and the happy rewards are yours. Welcome to the Fort William and Glen Coe area, one of the best walking areas in Britain.

Inchree Waterfalls

Start	Inchree, near Corran Ferry
Distance	3 miles (4.75km)
Approximate time	2 hours
Parking	Car park, Inchree
Refreshments	Tigh an Righ guest-house; Onich village
Ordnance Survey maps	Landranger 41 (Ben Nevis & Fort William) and Outdoor Leisure 38 (Ben Nevis & Glen Coe)

These falls are remarkably little known considering how close they lie to the busy A82 Glen Coe–Fort William road. Inchree and the Steall Falls (Walk 5) could well be visited in one day. The Forestry Commission has laid out two walks here, to take in a visit to the falls and also to use part of the old military road: easy walking with big rewards, following a mixture of both circuits.

The Inchree Waterfalls

Inchree is a forestry hamlet lying off the A82 between Onich and the Corran Ferry, and is clearly signposted. The minor village road ends at a car park at the point where the walks commence. They have been unobtrusively marked and benches are often available at strategic viewpoints.

The waterfall path skirts a field to a burn, then wanders across the hillside **Ⓐ**, a mix of rock, heather and gale (bog-myrtle; crush the leaves to release the aromatic scent). Passing through a gate you have a sudden first view of the fall. What is seen is only the top fall; the equally large lower one is seen only from a turning off to a viewpoint. Other falls further down are invisible but often audible, and at second and third viewpoints two smaller falls are seen above the top big one.

The path turns away from this watery extravagance and heads up to come out on to a forestry track. Turn left **Ⓑ** and follow the track downhill, a fine section of walk with views over the Corran Narrows of Loch Linnhe. Away to the south-west you may pick out distant Glensanda quarry which has supplied granite chips for the Channel Tunnel. Far off is the island of Mull. Seedling birches and various brooms grow on the bank beside the track.

The forest runs for many miles up Loch Linnhe. After several bends on the walk down, turn off the track to take a path, right **C**, which is clearly marked, though inaccurately called Wade's Road (it postdates Wade, although it was a military road). This heads up a wooded glade before crossing a burn, via a footbridge, to climb more steeply until the forest thins. The path is a bit muddy in places and also, for a while, has a base of white stone which is quartzite, the same rock that crowns Stob Bàn (Walk 26). When more open ground is reached, it can be seen that the hillside over on the right has lines along it, a bit like 'parallel roads' (see Walk 9). In fact they are the signs of lateral moraines from the period when Loch Linnhe was a huge glacier. Make sure you look back, as there is a fine view down to the sea.

The path eventually comes out to a forestry track beside an old quarry where you turn left by a red-marked post and a map board **D**. The military road goes straight on, and originally ran all the way to Fort William; the walk follows the forestry track, curving round to descend the next glen where, again, you have a sudden view of the sea, first over to Kentallen Bay and then down the length of Loch Linnhe. There are glimpses of the Inchree falls as you begin to descend more steeply.

At a slight bend in the track there is a Forest Walk sign where you turn off **E** to follow a path down through the trees. Some of the stepping-stones have a lovely sheen on them due to the mica in the rock. The path debouches at some buildings. Head left through these and a footpath beyond, marked by a red post, leads through to the car park.

Tigh an Righ guest-house, where the minor road rejoins the A82, offers day-long refreshments, and Onich village, with all facilities, is only about a mile (1.5km) off in the Glen Coe direction. ●

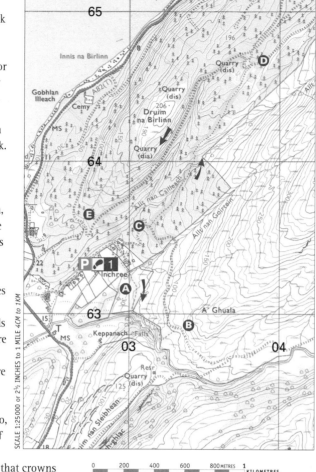

SCALE 1:25000 or 2½ INCHES to 1 MILE 4CM to 1KM

0 200 400 600 800 METRES 1 KILOMETRES
0 200 400 600 YARDS ½ MILES

Hospital Lochan, Glencoe

Start	Glencoe village
Distance	3 miles (4.75km)
Approximate time	2 hours
Parking	In Glencoe village
Refreshments	In Glencoe village
Ordnance Survey maps	Landranger 41 (Ben Nevis & Fort William), Outdoor Leisure 38 (Ben Nevis & Glen Coe)

This is a delightful walk to start or finish a day and offers a lush woodland setting, in great contrast to the ruggedness more usually encountered in Glen Coe. In early summer the rhododendrons will be in bloom, and early or late in the day the woods are fragrant and cool – and the views over loch, sea and hill are often sharper then.

Glencoe, the village, retains something of its ancient character. The walk begins by heading along its one street towards the dramatic form of the Pap of Glencoe (Walk 15). This was the old road through Glen Coe. The Celtic cross on the left is in memory of the men of Glencoe who lost their lives in the Great War of 1914–18. (Before you cross the River Coe by the fine humpback bridge, you might like to take the no-through road to the right to see the monument to MacIan, Chief of Glencoe, who fell with his people in the Massacre of Glencoe.)

Shortly after crossing the bridge turn left, up the hospital drive. At the point where the drive forks take the right, unsurfaced track which leads to a car park **A**. The Forestry Commission has created three local walks and this route more or less combines all of these in a single circuit.

Leave the car park in the far corner to get on to a steep gravel path twisting up through a jungle of *Rhododendron ponticum.* (You can see how efficiently this seeds; the plant has now become a menace in many areas.) There is a viewpoint here and then an even steeper pull up to the top of the hill **B**, the reward for which is an even more extensive view.

The path then descends almost as steeply and comes out on to a track beside the lochan. Turn right here to walk round the end of the lochan **C**, which is artificial, the work of Lord Strathcona who laid out these grounds and built the big house (now the hospital) in such a way as to try and 're-create' Canada for the sake of his half-Red-Indian wife. There is plenty of the Canadian flower *Gaultheria* growing by the path.

Walk on along the far side of the lochan. There are several overgrown islets and across the 'dam' can be seen a boathouse/shelter. A path goes off right **D**; take this for a new circuit, the Woodland Walk. Ignore the first path breaking off right, but several others (also to the right) are worth brief diversions as they lead on to ever-changing viewpoints. The path switch-backs along and, when it forks **E**, bear left and descend through another jungle of rhododendrons.

This comes out on a big track. Turn left and walk along to an arch formed by two intertwining rowan trees (a symbol of good luck), fronting a tiny lily-pond. The track forks at the arch **F**. Go right, up to the boathouse/shelter, cross over the 'dam' and turn left to pass the rowans again and so back along the drive towards a white house. Just before it (more or less opposite where this track was joined the first time) bear sharp left along a lower track which leads to the car park **A** and on back to the village.

The fjord-like nature of Loch Leven is well seen on this walk. The great ridges of Beinn a' Bheithir (Ben Vair) sweep down to the sea and the Ballachulish Bridge appears a tiny link over its narrows. The islands in front include Eilean Munde, the ancient burial site of the clan Macdonald. The grounds of Lord Strathcona's house evidently failed to re-create Canada to the

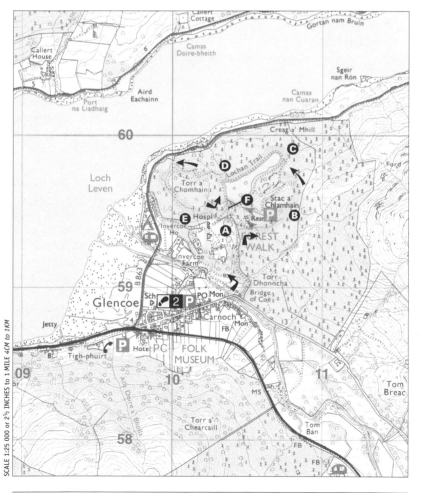

satisfaction of his wife, for the couple returned to British Columbia.

Once you are back in Glencoe village, take time to visit the Glencoe and North Lorne Folk Museum. The name Glen Coe is synonymous with the infamous Massacre of 1692 and that story is well illustrated here, as is much else relating to life in the glens in times past. Three miles (4.75km) up the glen's main road (A82) is the National Trust for Scotland Visitor Centre which has interpretative displays, refreshments, etc, though it is due to be relocated down the glen.

Hospital Lochan, Glencoe

Gondola Walks, Nevis Range

Start	Nevis Range gondola station
Distance	6 miles (9.5km), including all walks
Approximate time	4 hours, including all walks
Parking	Car park at gondola station
Refreshments	Snowgoose Restaurant, top station; café at lower station
Ordnance Survey maps	Landranger 41 (Ben Nevis & Fort William), Outdoor Leisure 38 (Ben Nevis & Glen Coe)

This is quite different from the other walks in this guide. The time given is for the walks, top and bottom, and the ride up and down in Britain's only mountain gondola system. This was built to serve the Aonach Mor ski-grounds, but incorporates a variety of summer services, including a high-level restaurant, shops, interpretative displays, etc. Two walks lead from the top station to viewing points, and at the foot two forest trails have been laid out. All are mentioned below, but which ones you walk is a matter of choice. Both walks at the top and one at the foot are described – but allow much more time to enjoy fully this unique experience. There is a café at the lower station, in addition to the Snowgoose at the top. One word of warning: the weather at the top station can be much colder, or can change rapidly, in comparison to the wooded, sheltered landscape below, so always take warm, protective clothing with you on the gondola walks. *The gondola is very popular, so early arrival is advisable. (Open 10am–5.30pm; 10.30am–7.30pm July, August.)*

Nevis Range lies off the A82; the turning to it (signposted) is about 4 miles (6.5km) along the route to Spean Bridge from Fort William. A 1½-mile drive (2.5km) through Leanachan Forest leads to the lower station, car parks, etc, from which the gondolas ply up the mountain. From little above sea-level at the foot, the spectacular ride takes you up to 2200ft (660m), where the Snowgoose Restaurant and other facilities are sited and where you can walk to two different viewpoints. These are well signposted and laid out with hard gravelly surfaces to minimise erosion of the fragile mountain vegetation. Nevis Range is a fine example of how development and conservation can work hand in hand.

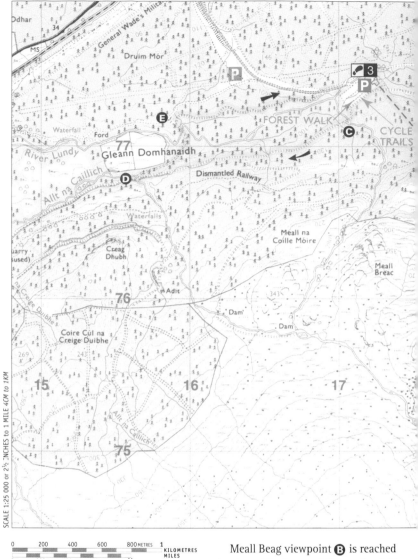

Sgurr Finnisg-aig viewpoint **A** is reached in about 20 minutes, being less than ½ mile (800m) from the top station; it is the prominent pointed knoll over to the left as seen from the ascending gondolas. This steep projecting hill gives wide views to the Great Glen and along to Roybridge, with, below, the vast sea of Leanachan Forest, one of the country's largest conifer plantings.

Meall Beag viewpoint **B** is reached in about 30 minutes. It lies to the right of the top station, along a hillside path. The far side is high above the deep pass separating the two Aonachs from Carn Mor Dearg and Ben Nevis. The Ben, Fort William, Loch Linnhe and Loch Eil can all be seen.

Having enjoyed one or both of these walks and refreshments in the Snowgoose, return to the foot of the mountain. Much of the area was clear-felled and has now been planted with a range of both deciduous and coniferous

The spectacular gondola lift, Nevis Range

species, so will form a beautiful woodland in a few years' time. The woodland walks allow visitors to see the forest growing, which will reward regular visits over the years ahead. The woodland walks start at the hillside side of the car park, at a Forestry Commission notice board.

Turn right and walk along the forestry track westwards to the first bridge, over the Allt Daim, which comes down the pass overlooked by the Meall Beag viewpoint. Here the two marked paths split **C**. A white-marked path breaks up left, but the walk you follow, a red-marked path, continues straight ahead.

This Gleann Domhanaidh Forest Walk is about 2 miles long (3.25km) and will take an hour to complete. It follows the forest track westwards to reach the next big stream coming down off the mountain, the Allt na Caillich, a wild and overgrown watercourse seen from the bridge. Just before you reach this bridge there is a turning area on the right and the walk takes the track from there **D** down to green fields. Cross the top field to a gap in the far wall. (Note what the trough at the fence is made from.) The path leads on down to a footbridge over the River Lundy and up to a forestry track. Turn right **E** to follow this through the felled area, and end with a footpath through mature trees to reach the corner of the car park by a footbridge. ●

Mamore Lodge

Start	Kinlochleven
Distance	3½ miles (5.5km)
Approximate time	2½ hours
Parking	In centre of Kinlochleven
Refreshments	Mamore Lodge, and in Kinlochleven
Ordnance Survey maps	Landranger 41 (Ben Nevis & Fort William), Outdoor Leisure 38 (Ben Nevis & Glen Coe)

This is a short walk but it climbs from sea-level to 820ft (250m) in the first mile (1.5km) of walking. In so doing it is following the line of Caulfeild's old military road and the start of the last day of the West Highland Way walk. Mamore Lodge offers refreshments, and a footpath leads back to Kinlochleven. The walk offers some of the same views as Walk 21 without being so demanding.

Head out of Kinlochleven on the B863 in the direction of Fort William till, opposite the school, the West Highland Way is clearly indicated **Ⓐ**. This path climbs up through birchwoods – which are particularly colourful in autumn – and offers fine views along Loch Leven to the Pap of Glencoe (Walk 15). Keep to the left when it forks, and soon the tarred drive to Mamore Lodge is crossed; eventually, as you clear the woods, the estate track from Mamore Lodge to the Lairigmor is joined **Ⓑ**. This is a fine viewpoint looking to the hills across Loch Leven – Garbh Bheinn and the Aonach Eagach.

Turn right to follow the track past a TV station with a mast until you reach Mamore Lodge, a hotel perched in a unique situation **Ⓒ** and where refreshments are available. Cedar trees and rhododendrons add an exotic air, and the spring scent of the yellow azaleas can be almost overpowering. The lodge was built for the landowner by the aluminium company when they built their works next to the previous lodge, in what is now Kinlochleven. King Edward VII was its most famous visitor (1909) and the Bibby family, of shipping fame, were long-time tenants. The estate actually belongs to the firm Alcan now, but sheep, deer and recreation are still its main activities. Walkers are often grateful to find that the lodge is now a welcoming hotel!

From the lodge head back up to continue along the 'private' road till it comes to the keeper's white house, kennels, etc. A footpath goes round to the right of this establishment. Just beyond, a knoll on the right seems to have a deer standing on its slope – but this proves to be man-made, a target in fact for trying rifles out before taking them on the hill. Just past the knoll is a large, cleared, flat space to the right and here the descent begins **Ⓓ**.

The path is rather unclear to begin with (a sign may be installed, however)

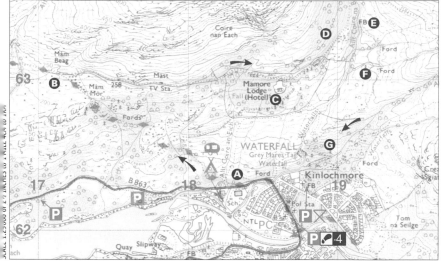

```
0    200   400   600   800 METRES  1
                                      KILOMETRES
                                      MILES
0    200   400   600 YARDS   ½
```

but start off down from the far side of the open area, to the right of the rubbish that has been tipped over the edge, and then swing left under this open area, with the path soon becoming clear as it angles down to the wooded depths of the Allt Coire na Bà. (The continuation on the other side can be seen clearly too.)

The burn is crossed by a gracefully arched stone bridge **E** but this is now in poor shape, with even some of the keystones gone from the roadway (you cross at your own risk!). There have been local calls to restore this fine work, and it is to be hoped that they succeed. Just downstream from the bridge is a superb deep swimming-pool, backed by a small fall.

The path angles up from the bridge, joins with other paths, crosses over a couple of streams, and then heads off more determinedly towards the town below **F**.

Before the final slope into town you will both hear and then see the famous Grey Mare's Fall **G** which is one of the grandest falls in Scotland. You can break off to reach its foot as it plunges, seemingly out of nowhere, into the deep-cut gorge. You should beware here as the wet rocks can be very slippery.

The path comes out between a church and a small car park. Turn right, then immediately left, on to a street which will lead to the B863 and the town centre. The church serves teas, and Kinlochleven has a wide range of facilities from a chip-shop to grand hotels. Across the River Leven, on the left, is the attractive Visitor Centre, where there are extensive displays telling the fascinating 'Aluminium Story'. It is open all year and admission is free. Walk 21 'The Heights of Kinlochleven' gives a little more detail on this unexpected presence in a remote Highland hamlet.

The track near Mamore Lodge

Nevis Gorge and Steall Falls

Start	Head of Glen Nevis road
Distance	3 miles (4.75km)
Approximate time	2½ hours
Parking	Car park at end of Glen Nevis road
Refreshments	None
Ordnance Survey maps	Landranger 41 (Ben Nevis & Fort William), Outdoor Leisure 38 (Ben Nevis & Glen Coe)

This popular short walk goes through a gorge, often described as Himalayan in character, to reach a verdant meadow backed by one of the country's most scenic waterfalls, the 'bridal veil' of An Steall Bàn. The path is rough, traverses steep, wooded slopes, and is fortunately not over-tidied, so the atmosphere of grandeur is unspoilt.

The drive up Glen Nevis from Fort William is full of character. Travel early, as the car park is often full later on. Stop briefly where the road swings left to cross the River Nevis. Below the bridge are the Lower Falls, and above lies the climbers' playground of the Polldubh Crags. Further on, the road squeezes between two arching Scots pines, where big boulders bear the scratch marks of passing glaciers. At the car park a remarkable long waterslide comes down the hill. In summer (though not on Sundays) a mobile refreshment kiosk may be present.

An Steall Bàn

The gorge footpath leaves from the car park where a signpost indicates that it is 15 miles (24km) to Corrour Station – which you see also on Walks 14, 18 and 20. (The remoteness of this station emphasises the wildness of the region.) The gorge is steeply wooded and the path rough in places with a touch of 'exposure' to it (the term climbers use for the sense of having nothing beneath them!)

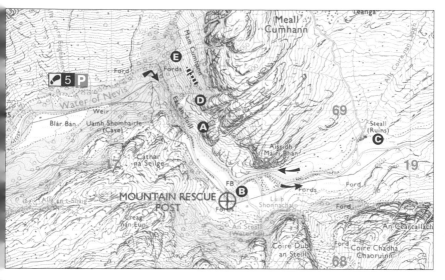

– all the more to impress the visitor. The water boils through, and the rocks are worn into many pots and cauldrons, some of which can be seen well up the crags, a clear indication of how the waters have carved their way down in the past.

The path suddenly comes out from the confines of the gorge **Ⓐ** (one steps down over a low wall) onto a big green meadow backed by the distant falls. Note the large crag, up to the left, which has clear marks of a water-channel on it, way above the present river level!

Follow the path up the edge of the meadow to gain a closer view of the falls, which at about 300ft (90m) are surpassed in height only by the Eas a' Chual Aluinn and the Falls of Glomach, neither of which can be seen so easily. The name *An Steall Bàn* means 'the white spout'. A bridge of just three strands of wire leads over to a cosy cottage which is a local climbing club's 'hut' **Ⓑ**. There is no necessity to cross (which will be a relief to the timid) unless you are determined to stand right below the falls.

A ten-minute walk up the glen brings you to a ruin (also called Steall) **Ⓒ** which is a good place to picnic and explore the river, the Allt Coire Guibhsachan, which comes down in a series of falls and clear pools – perfection on a midge-free, sunny day.

On the return look out for a track zigzagging up the spur above the gorge entrance **Ⓐ**. Very few walkers notice this alternative route out. (Those not sound of wind and limb are advised to return by the main path.) Turn right at the wall at the gorge mouth and along by some big boulders. After the fifth boulder turn left and you are on the clearly defined path which corkscrews up with sturdy determination till it comes level with the top of the gorge. Here a cairn marks this superb viewpoint **Ⓓ**. The name *Màm Cumhann* means 'narrow pass' and is clearly appropriate.

Continuing, take care on approaching the trees to follow the correct route. After the viewpoint the path swings right and is marked by a small cairn on a boulder. (Straight on is a false trail leading to difficulties.) It soon crosses a gully bed, wends on and, after another gully **Ⓔ**, descends steadily to rejoin the outward track. ●

Blackrock and Bà Bridge

Start	Blackrock, Rannoch Moor
Distance	6 miles (9.5km)
Approximate time	3 hours
Parking	Verges, Blackrock
Refreshments	Snack bar at ski lift car park; Kingshouse Hotel
Ordnance Survey maps	Landrangers 41 (Ben Nevis & Fort William) and 50 (Glen Orchy), Outdoor Leisure 38 (Ben Nevis & Glen Coe)

This is a walk on the western, Black Mount, edge of Rannoch Moor. Beyond the hills, westwards, is the Atlantic seaboard, yet the waters here drain east over the huge Moor to Rannoch and eventually, as the River Tay, enter the North Sea. The walk is not difficult but can catch bad weather, so choose a day of settled conditions before venturing into this wild and lonely corner. The views over the Moor are impressive; the distant cone in the east is the peak of Schiehallion.

Turn off the A82 at the road marked for White Corries, which is a winter ski resort although the ski-lift also operates in summer and is recommended as a follow-up to the walk. The start is opposite Blackrock, the pretty white cottage beside the road, with the triangular peak of the Buachaille Etive Mór looming behind it. Park wherever possible on the verges, taking care not to block any tracks or the entrance to Blackrock, which is a popular climbing 'hut' belonging to the Ladies' Scottish Climbing Club. If there is any real problem just go up to the ski-lift car park and walk down from there.

Head off along a rough track opposite Blackrock, taking the right fork at a junction (not marked on the map; the left fork leads to some huts). There is a West Highland Way post and a vehicle barrier across the track, which heads straight up the hillside. Beyond a

pretty, old bridge (part of the 18th-century military road) the track swings left **Ⓐ** and now traverses the hillside, gaining height steadily, with the view over the Moor growing ever more impressive and the A82 traffic reduced to the scale of toys.

On the hillside above the highest point on the track is a tall cairn, at 1450ft (450m) **Ⓑ**, erected to the memory of Peter Fleming. A tablet (missing because of vandalism?) bore the simple summary 'Author, Soldier and Traveller'. Ian Fleming (creator of James Bond) was Peter's brother and the family still owns the Blackmount estate. There is an extensive view from the cairn and the variety and scope of Rannoch Moor are evident, including the huge bowl of Coire Bà, down into

0	200	400	600	800 METRES	1	
						KILOMETRES
						MILES
0	200	400	600 YARDS	½		

Blackrock Cottage, Rannoch Moor

which the track now takes you. If the weather is deteriorating it might be wise to turn back from the cairn; Bà Bridge is still 2 miles (3.25km) away.

There are several bridges along the way before you come to the biggest, Bà Bridge, where the outward walk ends **C**. The River Bà here is picturesque and a good place to have a picnic. The more energetic can follow a path a little way up its north bank. Pools and small falls are inviting features.

Start off back to Blackrock along the track you came on. Soon an alternative will be followed which, by going higher, is even better for the sweeping views eastward. This higher line is that followed by the original military road, the outward route being a later track – along which all traffic ventured till the A82 was built in the 1930s.

The plantation on the left when you leave Bà Bridge occupies Drochaid and Carn an t-Saighdeir, the 'bridge' and 'cairn of the soldier'. A track off to the left a little further on leads to the ruin of Bà Cottage, once a less lonely spot but which declined with the arrival of the A82. Not far beyond this turning another path angles off, right, then turns to head east out to the A82 and Loch Bà. (This path can help pinpoint the turning off to the return route 300 yds later, on the left.)

The track rises steadily for this 300 yds until it reaches a bridge over the burn (which runs down to meet the A82 path at the point where it bends east). Immediately after this bridge (another fine one) turn left on to a barely discernible track **D**. This runs up on a bank beside the burn and becomes more recognisable as height is gained. The track then swings off right, climbing still, to round the hillside. The Fleming cairn lies below you this time.

The route then descends steadily. Some parts are a bit boggy but these are easily skirted. The Kingshouse Hotel lies some way ahead in a hollow, looking very much as it must have done when redcoats came marching along this way.

The outward route is rejoined at a point just above the first bridge mentioned **A**, and soon you reach Blackrock. If the weather is fair, a ride up the White Corries chairlift is recommended. It is open between 24 May and 15 September, from 10am to 5pm, and there is a snack bar at the car park. Afterwards a visit to the Kingshouse, the oldest inn in the country, may be welcome.

Loch Etive Shore Walk

Start	Foot of Glen Etive
Distance	6 miles (9.5km)
Approximate time	3 hours
Parking	Small car park, or off-road at Loch Etive jetty
Refreshments	None
Ordnance Survey maps	Landranger 50 (Glen Orchy), Outdoor Leisure 38 (Ben Nevis & Glen Coe)

This walk is all on rough (or wet) footpath in a remote area. Reaching the start involves an interesting 13-mile (20.75km) drive down a wild glen overlooked by spectacular hills. Ben Starav (Walk 27) dominates the head of the loch, a sea fjord which runs 18 miles (29km) from the tidal Falls of Lora at Connel Bridge to this remote spot. Boots, or better still Scandinavian mini-wellies, are essential if feet are to remain dry.

Visitors find it astonishing that a major loch like this can have no road along it, but in olden times the sea *was* the highway, and upper Glen Coe was

Highland stag

regularly approached via Loch Etive long before roads tackled Rannoch Moor. Turn off the A82 opposite the Kingshouse road end, signposted for Glen Etive, and twist down to arrive at a ruined pier near the head of the loch. (A motor vessel makes cruises up the loch from Taynuilt in summer but does not call at the pier.)

The path running along the west side of the loch reaches Bonawe after 11 miles (17.5km) but the present route will only wander down for about 3 miles (5km) – and the same back again. There is no habitation in that distance. The granite bulk of Ben Starav, 3541ft (1078m) high, guards the east side of Loch Etive. Above the path is Beinn Trilleachan, 2752ft (839m), offering a challenging ascent for the walker and one of the finest rock-climbing areas in the British Isles. You may well see climbers on the Trilleachan Slabs. After 1½ miles (2.5km) there is a small point, Aird

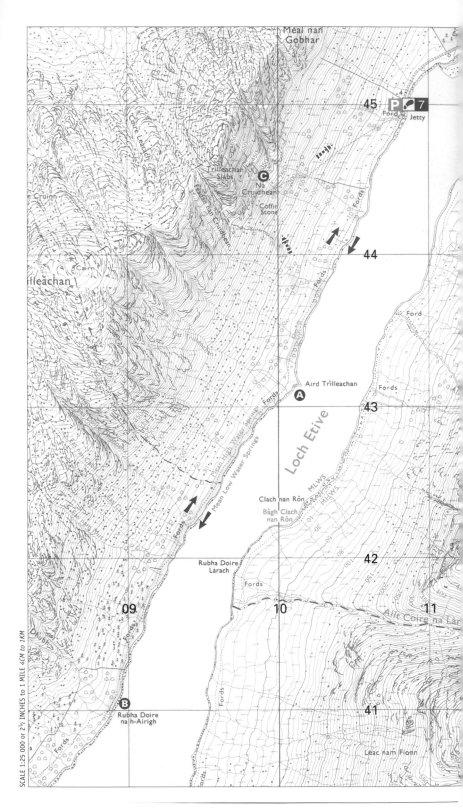

SCALE 1:25 000 or 2½ INCHES to 1 MILE *4CM to 1KM*

Méal nan
Gobhar

45 **P** 🚻 **7**
Ford   Jetty

Coire Làcach

Trìlleachan
Slabs

C
Na
Cruidhean

Coffin
Stone

44

-Cruinn

Ford

-illeachan

Cairn

Aird Trìlleachan   Fords

A

43

Loch Etive

Fords

Mean High Water Springs

MLWS

Mean Low Water Springs

Clach nan Ròn   MLWS
Bàgh Clach
nan Ròn

Fords

Rubha Doire
Làrach

42

Fords

09   10   11

Allt Coire na Làr

Dhubh-

Fords

B

Rubha Doire
na h-Airigh   41

Fords

Leac nam Fionn

Looking down Glen Etive to Cruachan

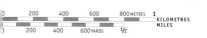

Trilleachan **A**. The path as far as there is exceptionally wet; don't be put off.

These first few miles have a scattering of natural woodlands (birch, oak, hazel, holly, etc), a remnant reminding that Scotland once was a forest country (and red deer were forest creatures) before we felled, burnt and destroyed our woodland heritage. Loch Etive has often been compared to Norway on account of its mix of woodland, water and rocky hills – and the abundant wildlife.

Three miles' (5km) walking **B** will give a good idea of this woody lochside, and a picnic or swim on the shore can be enjoyed before you head back again. (The route continuing south soon runs into thicker woodland and then vast plantations.) To avoid the very wet stretch it is possible to wander up towards the foot of the Trilleachan Slabs **C** (which is also worth doing if climbers are in action) and then follow a path down from there back to the ruined jetty. If the views impressed on the drive down Glen Etive, then the drive up is even better. The Two Passes (Walk 17), glaciated U-shaped valleys, show up well. The River Etive has scores of attractive small falls. ●

Caledonian Canal

Start	Gairlochy
Distance	8 miles (12.75km)
Approximate time	3½ hours
Parking	Limited roadside parking at Gairlochy
Refreshments	Moorings Hotel, Neptune's Staircase
Ordnance Survey maps	Landranger 41 (Ben Nevis & Fort William), Pathfinder 264, NN 08/18 (Glen Loy)

A canal cannot but offer gentle walking, but when the canal lies in the huge tear fault of the Great Glen (Glen Albyn), the walking is rather special. There is a great feeling of quietude in this area, and the views are spacious and grand, with the imposing form of Ben Nevis filling the view away to the south. The return walk along the B8004 offers even wider views. Traffic on the canal provides an added interest and the flight of locks called Neptune's Staircase, at Banavie, is an engineering masterpiece which is well worth visiting afterwards.

The Commando Memorial marks the point at which the B8004 leaves the A82 above Spean Bridge and leads down to Gairlochy. Gairlochy is not a town but simply a double set of locks where the canal enters Loch Lochy; they form one of the three major lock systems of the Caledonian Canal. The canal is 66 miles (106km) long in all, but only 22 miles (33km) of its length are true canal, the rest being spread over Loch Ness, Loch Oich and Loch Lochy. (Walk 24 starts at the locks at the north end of Loch Lochy.)

The canal was first surveyed in 1773 by James Watt but it took all the skills of Thomas Telford to construct it, between 1803 and 1847. Telford was often based at Gairlochy and his house still stands beside the locks. Today pleasure craft and fishing boats are the main users of the canal, though you may be lucky and see a fine sailing ship

going through. A plaque by the swing-bridge commemorates a Royal embarkation in 1958. The canal towpath is on the south-east side. Parking is limited so arrive early; some off-road spaces can be found above the locks to the west. Take care not to obstruct any of the entrances, as they are all used regularly.

At the start of the walk the River Lochy is close on the left. In order to build the locks Telford cut a new course for the waters of Loch Lochy so that they fell into the Spean at Mucomir, and this cut has since been turned into a small hydro scheme. Moy is the first landmark on the walk, where the swing-bridge Ⓐ crossing the canal is an old cast-iron structure, a unique feature. On the far side, just before the bridge, you may spot an intake, one of the water supplies that keep the canal topped up.

At Glen Loy (B) the canal crosses the River Loy, with a big arch to cope with spates and side arches for farm traffic. The Young Pretender and his newly gathered Jacobite army marched down Glen Loy after the standard had been raised at Glenfinnan. Care is needed for eventually leaving the canal, which runs high above Torcastle, left, and the roadside hamlet of Sheangain, right, neither visible at this point. The canal makes a bend to the right and widens. Keep an eye open for a telegraph pole on the bank with a number tag 837 on it, and a good path leads down from there (C). The three arches which take

Swing-bridge at Moy, on the Caledonian Canal

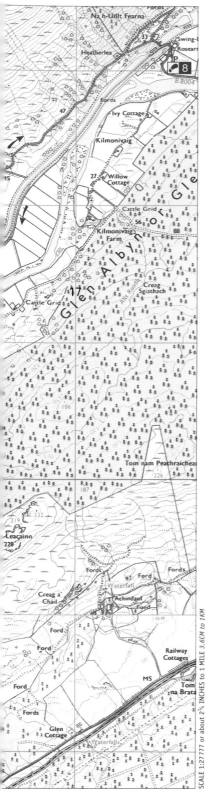

SCALE 1:27 777 or about 2¼ INCHES to 1 MILE 3.6CM to 1KM

farm track and stream under the canal are all of equal size and are shaped in the same section as the canal itself. On the other side a weir and boulders in the burn help to control spates.

It is interesting to note in passing that Torcastle is associated with Banquo – he was in fact a real person, though nowadays he is perhaps better known for his place in Shakespeare's *Macbeth*. Torcastle was once the seat of Clan MacIntosh, but the building is now a complete ruin.

When the track leading north from the canal reaches the tarred road, the B8004 **D**, turn right to follow it all the way back to the start; it is a very pleasant road which frequently gives splendid panoramic views of the surrounding area. In high summer watch out for speeding cars which can be a hazard along this stretch of road – if it turns out to be too busy, return by way of the canal towpath. At Loy **B** a rough track just before the road bridge leads down to the right, and here you can view the canal aqueduct and its sturdy arches.

If you drive back along the B8004 after you have completed the walk you can see one of the most impressive flights of locks to be found in Britain, at Banavie. The eight locks of Neptune's Staircase lift the level of the canal by a total of 64ft (19.2m). The lock-keepers' houses were built with big bay windows for easy observation of the canal proceedings and they still stand, on the west bank. The Moorings Hotel is recommended for refreshments at this point. A mile further on, the canal enters the sea at another pleasant spot, which can be reached on foot from Banavie or by driving round by Corpach on the A830. ●

Parallel Roads, Glen Roy

Start	Brae Roy Lodge
Distance	8½ miles (13.5km)
Approximate time	3½ hours
Parking	Roadside, before Brae Roy Lodge
Refreshments	None
Ordnance Survey maps	Landranger 34 (Fort Augustus & Glen Albyn) and Pathfinder 251, NN 29/39 (Laggan)

The Parallel Roads are one of nature's freak features and well worth a visit. The time given above is only for the walk itself, along to the White Falls (Eas Ban); there will be several stops during the drive up the narrow, twisty road, to look at the Parallel Roads, so allow a whole morning or afternoon out and back from Roybridge. The walking is mostly on farm tracks. Do not stray off the described route in the stalking season, and try not to disturb sheep, especially in the lambing season (May), when dogs should be left behind.

Leave the A86 Glen Spean road at Roybridge to take a minor road up the west side of Glen Roy. There are hairpin bends and dangerous corners on this narrow road, so caution is required. When the hamlet of Bohuntine is passed more open ground begins, and

above a long, sweeping bend there is a car park. Pull in here for a first look at the Parallel Roads.

These are well named, as a succession of roads seem to run along the hillsides. During the Ice Ages a huge glacier dammed the foot of the

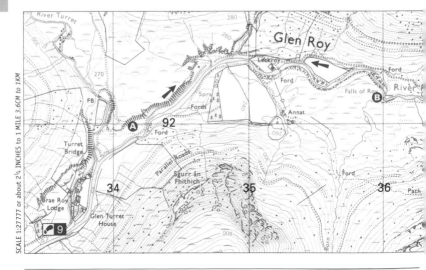

glen and a natural reservoir occurred. The Parallel Roads are simply the variable shorelines of this reservoir. (If you actually want to set foot on them you can climb up the slope above the car park.) Continue to the end of the public road and be sure to park *before* Brae Roy Lodge so as not to obstruct farm movement.

Walk on up the glen. A humpback bridge crosses the Turret, with a road heading left. Keep to the right fork, following the River Roy . Note the huge flat-topped areas above you which are the eroded tables of glacial deposits. The track stays on the north bank but a short diversion is recommended to see the Falls of Roy **B**. The track then climbs the knobbly Creagan na Gaoithe ('windy crags') to reach a remote strath with a lonely

bothy, Luib-chonnal, at the far side **C**. The track may not be helpful, as it is often eroded by the river, and it is best to keep along the hillside before aiming down to the bothy. This recently needed some work, as the Allt Chonnal was cutting away the bank at the east gable. Facing the bothy are the White Falls (Eas Ban), an attractive plunge into a pool which is good for swimming.

Luib-chonnal is the natural turning place and the falls a good place for a picnic. (It is particularly important to leave no litter, which could endanger grazing deer.) On the return walk there are still constant views of the Parallel Roads, which cross every hillside, and make this route unique. ●

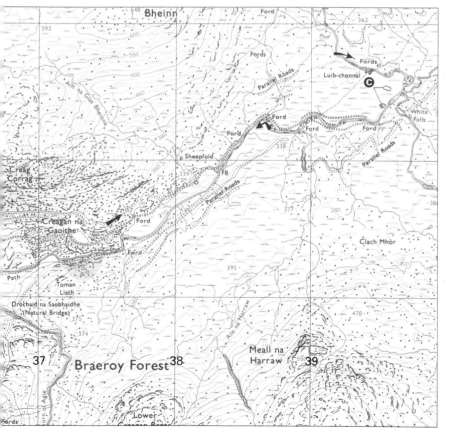

Arkaig Glens

Start	Eas Chia-aig (waterfall)
Distance	7 miles (11.25km)
Approximate time	3½ hours
Parking	Eas Chia-aig car park
Refreshments	None
Ordnance Survey maps	Landranger 34 (Fort Augustus & Glen Albyn), Pathfinders 264, NN 08/18 (Glen Loy), and 250, NN 09/19 (Loch Arkaig)

This is a lonely but easy enough walk which takes in an 1444-ft (440m) pass to link the outward and returning glens. The start and finish lie by a delightful waterfall, and there are some splendid and varied views and a real sense of wilderness. Go well-shod and equipped as for hill-climbing. The walk should not be attempted in heavy rain. During the stalking season, the walk should be limited to the first section (Gleann Cia-aig).

Above Spean Bridge turn off on to the B8004 at the Commando Memorial, descend to Gairlochy and the Caledonian Canal, then turn right through woodlands to Loch Lochy side, before turning sharply west at Clunes along the Mile Dorcha, the Dark Mile. This is actually nearer two miles long, and links Loch Lochy and Loch Arkaig. Just before you reach Loch Arkaig there is a car park on the right which is the starting point of the walk. Beside the car park are the stepped falls of the Chia-aig (pronounced *caig*), the waters of which pour down into the peat-dark Witches Pool. The best view is from the road bridge.

Note that if the river is in spate the route given below should be walked only as far as ⓑ, since the ford there should not be attempted in these conditions.

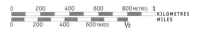

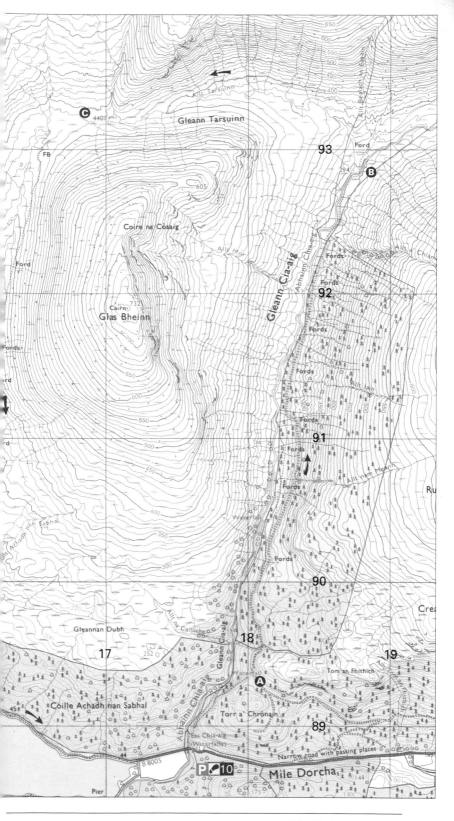

A footpath starting from the right-hand side of the car park heads steeply up through the forest, following the river initially and then bearing right to come out on a forestry road **A**. Turn left along this road. There is one gate with a high stile early on and after a mile (1.5km) the plantation is left for more natural woodlands up Gleann Cia-aig. The last stretch has no trees and leads to a bridge which is dangerously decayed, so the Abhainn Chia-aig has to be forded **B**. The continuation should be avoided in the stalking season.

The fine tributary coming down Gleann Tarsuinn to the west is the next stage: a stream with many small falls and pools, held in a deep glen between steep hills. Follow the north bank, crossing many side-streams. The going is trackless and steep but the watershed is due west **C** (infant streams come in from both north and south), and keeping on westwards leads to the Allt Dubh, which is simply followed down to Loch Arkaig at Achnasaul. There is a roughly made track down the glen.

Be sure to keep strictly to the route when the fields are reached, and close all gates to keep the sheep and cattle from escaping (the high fence is to keep the deer *out*). The path crosses a burn to reach the fenced-off slopes at a gate **D**, but becomes indistinct beyond. Aim straight ahead from the gate, towards a green knoll with trees. Pass left of the knoll, cross another burn, and go straight on (over a slight rise) to descend to the gate leading out of the grazing fields **E**. Achnasaul lies up to the left, and the building off to the right is a salmon farm.

Follow the undulating tarred road back to the car park, which is reached after about 1½ miles (2.5km). Traffic is light and walkers are few, so be on the lookout for unexpected vehicles. ●

The shores of Loch Arkaig

On to Rannoch Moor

Start	Rannoch Station
Distance	8 miles (12.75km)
Approximate time	4 hours
Parking	Nearest: Bridge of Orchy and Tulloch stations
Refreshments	Café at station; Moor of Rannoch Hotel
Ordnance Survey maps	Landrangers 41 (Ben Nevis & Fort William) and 42 (Glen Garry & Loch Rannoch), Outdoor Leisure 38 (Ben Nevis & Glen Coe), and Pathfinder 307, NN 45/55 (Loch Rannoch, West)

This is an easy walk, to be kept for a sunny summer day when the utter loneliness of Rannoch Moor can be savoured to the full. A run on the popular West Highland Line starts and ends the day (Bridge of Orchy and Tulloch are the most convenient stations for motorists). Most of the route is along forestry track, but the Moor stands at a height of 1000ft (300m) and the weather can be inhospitable at times.

Rannoch Station may be approached by road, but not from the west, as this is where Rannoch Moor sprawls in an empty area about the size of the Lake District. There is simply a lonely hotel, a café on the station platform, and a few houses. The line northwards heads off over an impressive viaduct. The big stone carving of Mr Renton commemorates one of the railway company directors who, as a private benefactor, assisted with the costs of the railway's construction when financial difficulties arose. The navvies manhandled a boulder on to the platform and sculpted the likeness using only the tools of their trade.

Leave the station by its exit over the footbridge which leads to a car park. The Moor of Rannoch Hotel lies beyond, and before that a SRWS sign indicates our route: 'Glencoe by Loch Laidon'. Cross the railway by the track which then bends round the Dubh Lochan, which is a small extension, as it were, to the length of Loch Laidon. The track is followed just outside the forest edge, passing above a white house, to a fork level with the end of Loch Laidon proper; the right-hand fork is taken, leading into the forest. A high stile gives access as the gate is locked Ⓐ.

Rannoch Moor

Follow the track through the forest. Eventually it climbs steadily to a gate (open, so there is no stile), and after another five minutes' walking ends at a turning place. The turning place was once across the stream but past spates have cut off the chance of vehicles going any further. On the original turning place over the stream a signpost indicates the continuation: 'Public footpath to Glencoe' **B**.

This is a grand viewpoint. The real scale of Loch Laidon is seen and yet Rannoch Moor extends for the same distance again to the south-west, while over the hills on the other side of the loch lie further vast reaches of the Moor. The continuation path descends steeply towards the loch to reach the line of power poles; turn right **C** to

follow these along through the forest break, a route which has no made path and can be decidedly wet. (Before heading off along this line, however, make sure you thoroughly register where the path heads up to the turning place **B**, or the return journey may entail complications!)

There is a mile (1.5km) of this forest route before a gate with a stile leads out to the open country beyond. The line of poles is still followed, the path dipping and rising across a hollow with crags higher up the slope, and gradually beginning to head west. A mile (1.5km) out from the forest there is a stream, the Allt Riabhach na Bioraich ('speckled

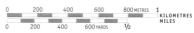

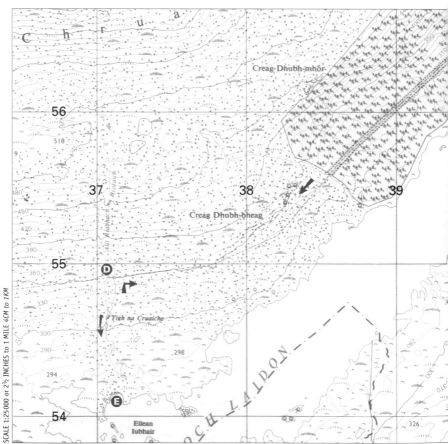

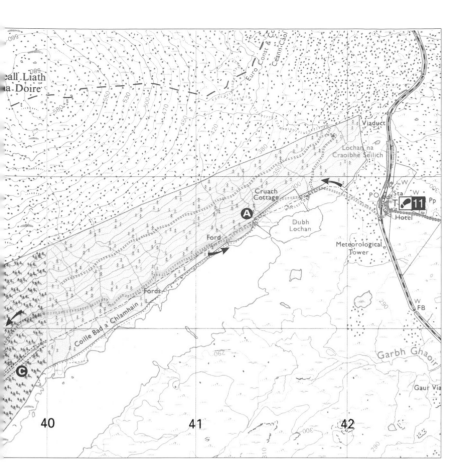

stream of the heifer'), which is followed down **D** past the ruined site of Tigh na Cruaiche ('house of the gathering place' – where there was once a drovers' stance) to reach the journey's end on the lonely shore of Loch Laidon **E**.

The granite sands can dazzle on a sunny day and in spring the calling of greenshanks and divers can be quite eerie in such utter solitude. The everyday world seems very remote. The islands out in the loch are tree-covered because they lie beyond the reach of grazing deer. One island is called Eilean Iubhair, 'yew tree island'. Once much of the Highlands was tree-covered, as the bleached flares of old tree-stumps in the bog prove, but overgrazing and misuse have made them a wet desert.

Having enjoyed this quiet spot and used half the 'between trains' time,

return by the same route, following the line of the poles. Be careful not to overshoot the path up to the good forest track **C**. If you do, the burn or the fence should indicate that you have passed the spot and should back-track to the turning. Hopefully this path will soon be signposted. Thereafter the track is followed back to Rannoch Station, which can be seen from the turning place at the track's end **B**. The wedge of hill, on the horizon right of the station, is Schiehallion.

The tearoom at the station and the Moor of Rannoch Hotel will offer welcome refreshments until it is time for the train – or maybe you will be tempted to stay and take the train the next day for the walks (14, 18 and 20) which start at Corrour, the next stop up the line towards Fort William. ●

Cameron Country

Start	East end of Loch Arkaig
Distance	7 miles (11.25km)
Approximate time	3½ hours
Parking	Eas Chia-aig car park
Refreshments	None
Ordnance Survey maps	Landranger 34 (Fort Augustus & Glen Albyn) and Pathfinder 264, NN 08/18 (Glen Loy)

This is a walk into a completely unspoilt, remote corner of the hills west of the Great Glen (Glen Albyn). The walking is on farm-type road but the visitor could enjoy a whole day in this area with its unusual peace and quiet. Because the motor road along Loch Arkaig is a dead end, few motorists seek it out, and Glen Mallie is similarly remote, so this is a connoisseur's choice. Keep it for a sunny day of blissful ease. Be particularly careful not to leave litter.

The time given above is simply the basic walking time, but the area defies hurry. Even the motor approach calls for care. Loch Arkaig is the heart of Clan Cameron country and the setting of D.K. Broster's novels, and a relaxed pace will allow a true appreciation of its atmosphere. The B8004 is taken from the Commando Memorial above Spean Bridge down to Gairlochy, the locks over the Caledonian Canal (the start of Walk 8); then turn right through beautiful woodlands by Loch Lochy before turning sharp west at Clunes along the Mile Dorcha, the Dark Mile, to reach Loch Arkaig itself. Park in the car park on the right beside the attractive stepped waterfall, the Eas Chia-aig, where Walk 10 also starts.

Head west towards the end of the loch and turn left on to the Achnacarry drive just before the loch is reached. Once across the bridge turn right **Ⓐ** to walk for 2 miles (3.25km) through

mixed woodlands above the waters of Loch Arkaig. This leads to the green meadows where Glen Mallie runs down to the loch; the lushness of this area is

due to the rich alluvial soil here. The cottage (Inver Mallie), overhung by bird cherries, is a bothy – an abandoned cottage used as a refuge **B**. Garrons (Highland ponies) may be wandering about here, and there is also a wide variety of birdlife.

Return by the same route, but at the junction at the east end of Loch Arkaig **A** instead of turning left keep on along the road ahead, which runs down to Achnacarry, home of Cameron of Locheil, the clan chieftain. The house is not open to the public but there is an interesting Clan Cameron Museum in the old post office building **C**. This is open in the afternoons from mid-April to mid-October. Achnacarry was the centre for wartime commando training – hence the memorial up at the A82. More information on this story is on display in the Spean Bridge Tourist

The Eas Chia-aig

Office. For the walker returning to Loch Arkaig and the car park this wartime activity will seem strangely incongruous amid such quiet and peaceful surroundings. ●

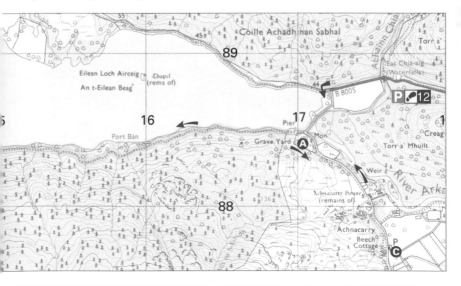

The Stalker's Path on Beinn na Caillich

Start	Layby on B863 ½ mile (800m) west of Kinlochleven
Distance	7½ miles (12km)
Approximate time	4½ hours
Parking	At start
Refreshments	None
Ordnance Survey maps	Landranger 41 (Ben Nevis & Fort William), Outdoor Leisure 38 (Ben Nevis & Glen Coe)

This shapely hill on the northern shore of Loch Leven dominates the view for walkers on the final section of the West Highland Way from Kinlochleven to Fort William. The steep climb to the summit is eased by a fine stalker's path, which may be boggy in places, but the short-cropped turf of the ridge beyond offers delightful walking with panoramic views. If you intend to walk this route in the stalking season (August to late October), contact the Mamore and Grey Corries Hillphone Service on 01855 831511.

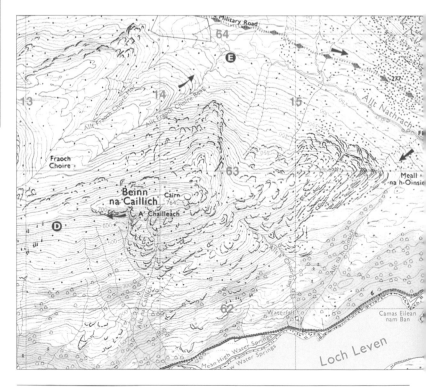

From the layby, walk west along the road for about 200 yds (183m), passing the drive to Mamore Lodge Hotel, then turn right on the obvious stony path that leads through a gap in the fence and onto the hillside. The path wanders up through bracken and open birch woods and after 10 minutes' climb it joins the West Highland Way 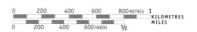. Turn left and follow the well-made path, which is part of the Stirling to Fort William military road built between 1748 and 1753 under the direction of Major William Caulfeild. As the path zigzags up, the views open out, along Loch Leven to the Pap of Glencoe, and back towards Kinlochleven.

After another 15 minutes the route levels out and joins the vehicle track from Mamore Lodge to the Lairigmor **B**. The going is easy now, with the conical peak of Beinn na Caillich dominating the view; the stalker's path that will take you to the summit is clearly visible on the right flank of the ridge. After ½ mile (800m), soon after crossing a small wooden bridge, keep your eyes peeled for a narrow path that leads down to the left past a power-line pole **C**. Follow this indistinct and boggy path down to a wooden footbridge over the Allt Nathrach.

From the bridge the stalker's path zigzags comfortably up the steep, heathery, eastern nose of Beinn na Caillich. A steady climb of 30 minutes leads to the shoulder of the ridge, where the path continues less distinctly, before once again zigzagging up to the right of the final steep summit cone. The path continues in a rising traverse across the northern side of the summit, past a tiny lochan, and then climbs to the left and peters out in a grassy depression on the summit ridge; of the two cairns on either side, the one to the right (west) is the higher.

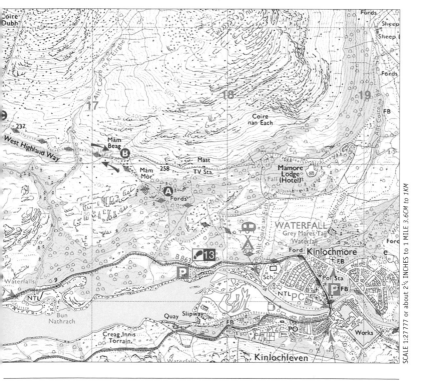

SCALE 1:27777 or about 2¼ INCHES to 1 MILE 3.6CM to 1KM

On a sunny summer's day the summit provides a superb picnic spot, with springy, short-cropped turf and magnificent views. To the south across the loch are the Glen Coe hills and Beinn a' Bheithir; to the west lie Loch Linnhe and the distant ridges of Morvern and Ardgour; the bulk of Ben Nevis looms beyond the pink and grey screes of the Mamores to the north; and to the east Kinlochleven nestles beneath the moors around the Blackwater Reservoir.

Continue west along the delightful grassy ridge, taking care not to approach too closely the steep drop to the south. After ½ mile (800m), at the first saddle in the ridge **D**, drop directly down the even grassy slope on the north side and, when the slope eases off, bear right along the heathery dip that follows the line of the Allt Fraoch Choire Beag. Traces of an indistinct path will be found on the right bank of the tiny stream, but when the burn drops into a steep V-shaped valley cross over to the left bank. Follow a faint path through the heather onto the ridge to the left of the burn and descend towards the meeting of the Allt Fraoch Coire Beag and Mór; the going is little rough here in the trackless heather, but fortunately it is all downhill.

When you reach the valley floor at the confluence of the streams **E**, cross the burn and climb the far bank to rejoin the West Highland Way. Turn right and follow the road back to the junction at **B**, then retrace the outward route back to the starting point, taking care to watch for the inconspicuous junction at **A**, just before a bridge with an iron handrail.

Beinn na Caillich from the West Highland Way

Round Loch Ossian

Start	Corrour Station
Distance	9 miles (14.5km)
Approximate time	4½ hours
Parking	None (nearest: Tulloch Station)
Refreshments	None
Ordnance Survey maps	Landrangers 41 (Ben Nevis & Fort William) and 42 (Glen Garry & Loch Rannoch), Outdoor Leisure 38 (Ben Nevis & Glen Coe), Pathfinder 292, NN 46/56 (Lower Loch Ericht)

Corrour Station lies at a height of 1340ft (400m) and Loch Ossian is one of the largest lochs to be found at such altitude. A walk round Loch Ossian is a rewarding expedition to follow from the West Highland Line, which for the purposes of this guide can be joined at any station from Bridge of Orchy to Fort William. The nearest station available to motorists is Tulloch. There is an idyllic youth hostel at the west end of Loch Ossian and a bunkhouse at Corrour Station. Walks 18 and 20 both start at Corrour as well, and combining some of these would make an interesting extended venture.

Corrour Station is often described as the most remote in Britain. There is no public road to it and apart from the bunkhouse, the youth hostel, and the shooting lodge at the other end of Loch Ossian, the area is quite uninhabited. Setting off from Corrour has a distinctive and rather exciting flavour.

Head off from the station eastwards along the estate track, ignoring a left fork **Ⓐ**, and in a mile (1.5km) you reach the first turning to the youth hostel situated at the water's edge. If you are lucky you may see handsome stags nearby. As you walk on there is a second turning to the hostel, at a 'crossroads' **Ⓑ**. The hostel is a former boat-house. The station was private till 1934; it was built for the estate owners, whose guests were brought to the loch by pony-trap before transferring to a steam yacht for the trip to the lodge.

At the crossroads take the path heading south (away from the loch) which follows a higher route and so greatly expands the range of the view.

Reflections on Loch Ossian

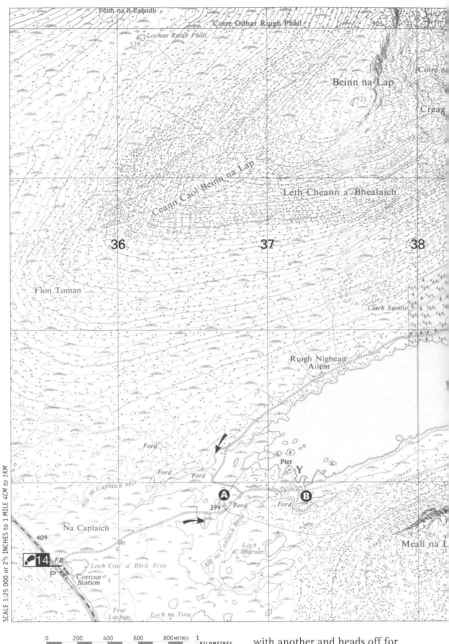

This path soon swings round until it is parallel with the lochside track but running at a higher level; it forms part of the old 'Road to the Isles' of song and legend. A bit wet in places, it steadily gains height. There is a gate and then, further up, the path merges

with another and heads off for Rannoch. There is a memorial plaque on a boulder at the merging of paths. Turn left at this junction **C** and follow the track down by the forest to join up with the lochside main track again **D**.

Continue along the main track. The distant U-shaped valley leads to the wild country of Ben Alder. The eastern slopes of the loch have been somewhat

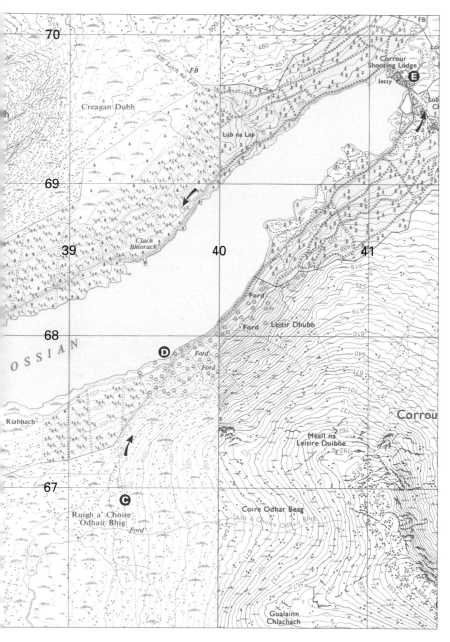

engulfed by conifers but Corrour Lodge at the end of Loch Ossian **E** has a delightful setting. Remnants of old gardens mean a dash of rhododendron colours in early summer.

The track back round the loch on the north shore is obvious. There is a memorial stone at the junction in the north corner. The right branch eventually leads out to Loch Laggan, but is an estate road only. The left branch eventually comes out of the plantation and completes the circuit of the loch through a bleaker landscape under the slopes of Beinn na Lap, 3073ft (937m). Turn right **A** to walk back to the station, which remains strangely invisible till close at hand. Leum Uilleim (Walk 18) lies anchored out in Rannoch Moor to the west. ●

Pap of Glencoe

Start	Glencoe village
Distance	5 miles (8km)
Approximate time	3½ hours
Parking	In Glencoe village
Refreshments	In Glencoe village
Ordnance Survey maps	Landranger 41 (Ben Nevis & Fort William) and Outdoor Leisure 38 (Ben Nevis & Glen Coe)

The Pap of Glencoe is one of the great landmark hills in this area and, as such, is a superlative viewpoint. The final slopes are rocky, and the climb is alternately rough, cloying and heathery. However, the ascent is relatively modest, though ironically it involves a steep climb and is therefore quite demanding.

As the old Glen Coe road offers limited parking it is most convenient to park in the village and walk the mile along to the start of the ascent. Once the forest on the left ends there is a kissing-gate leading through cattle pens to the hillside (do not take the tarred drive of Laraichean) and a rough service track for water intake-dams above **Ⓐ**. Follow this and when it forks keep right, to cross the burn. The track traverses to a dam on the next stream. A path heads uphill beside the obvious gully which leads towards the col **Ⓑ**, between the Pap and the ridge along to Sgorr nam Fiannaidh. From the col a rougher scramble leads up the final quartzite cone of this fine summit **Ⓒ**.

The summit gives a great feeling of height, as peaks overlooking water tend to do (Ben Nevis itself is not any more impressive), and the

sweeping view of Loch Leven to the east, and the Ballachulish narrows and bridge leading the eye to rugged Ardgour to the west, is a special experience, quite apart from the view up Glen Coe. Here the dominant peak is Bidean nam Bian, at 3766ft (1141m) the highest hill in Argyll. To the west can also be seen the sweeping ridges of complex Beinn a' Bheithir, which towers above Walk 16. All the local mountains rise steeply from near sea-

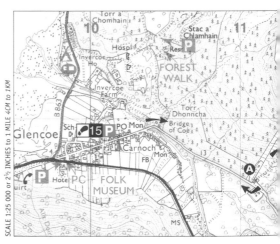

SCALE 1:25 000 or 2½ INCHES to 1 MILE 4CM to 1KM

level, and in the past made intimidating barriers to travel – people like the Wordsworths, Coleridge and Dickens have left diary accounts about Glen Coe that make it sound like Patagonia.

The Gaelic name for this summit is Sgorr na Ciche, *ciche* being a translation of 'pap' or 'breast'. It is rather more colloquial in the original, the Victorians having been careful to tone down or even change names such as this or Devil's Point (in the Cairngorms) to avoid the embarrassingly explicit.

Sgorr nam Fiannaidh, neighbouring Munro to the Pap, translates as 'peak of the Fianna'; the Fianna were the Fingalians, mythological warriors whose mighty deeds were told in tales of Finn MacCool. Ossian's Cave, seen from the road on the car journey up Glen Coe, is named after the bardic son of Fingal, and Glen Etive features in the great love story of Deirdre and Naoise, but the stories are common heritage and given sites all over Ireland and the Scottish Highlands.

Due south a track may be made out running into the hills up Gleann Leac na Muidhe, the 'glen of the slab of the

A winter view of the Pap of Glencoe

churn', a name whose explanation has been lost (as has so much) with the disappearance of the original population. The house at the road-end was that of the chief MacIan, who was the main target of the Massacre of Glencoe. Though an old man he was butchered, and his wife died from being so ill treated (her fingers were cut off to steal the rings she wore). The population was scattered in clachans (hamlets) all over the area and many either escaped up side-valleys or died in the blizzards trying to do so.

Descend by the same route, taking care on the rough, steep ground. From the col **B** you largely follow the Allt a' Mhuilinn, the 'stream of the mill' – a common name, as many streams like this once had mills on them. After entering the village over the bridge at the end of the walk, turn left for a moment to have a look at the monument to the Massacre.

This ascent could well be combined with Walk 2. An early ascent is recommended, to catch the morning freshness, then perhaps a drive to the Glen Coe (NTS) Visitor Centre for the historical aspects, and finally the Hospital Lochan walk for the evening colours over Ardgour. ●

A Ballachulish Walk

Start	Ballachulish
Distance	7 miles (11.25km)
Approximate time	3½ hours
Parking	Car park, Ballachulish
Refreshments	In Ballachulish
Ordnance Survey maps	Landranger 41 (Ben Nevis & Fort William) and Outdoor Leisure 38 (Ben Nevis & Glen Coe)

This short walk explores something of Ballachulish and traces part of an old drovers' (and pre-roads) route to Appin and Benderloch, the rich lands by the shores of Loch Linnhe. The return offers fine views over Loch Leven.

There is a car park, signposted, sited behind the information centre in Ballachulish. The A82 now bypasses the village but the turn-off is indicated.

Ballachulish was once famous for its slate quarries and the information centre has an excellent interpretative display on the subject which is worth seeing first, as it will add interest to the walk thereafter. Ballachulish was one of the last working slate quarries in Scotland (it closed in 1955), but remedial work (reseeding, replanting, and shifting spoil, in 1978–9) has largely removed the evidence of this, as is the case with the attractive railway line which once linked Ballachulish with Oban via Appin and Benderloch. The present walking route predates, and has outlasted, all these.

Walk seawards to see the tiny harbour which, like the hotel and the land itself, is all created out of quarry waste material. Boat trips operate in summer and you might be tempted to go on one on the return. Ballachulish has plenty of facilities and accommodation and would make a pleasant base in the area.

Head back and cross the road beyond the information centre to walk up through East Laroch, where there are shops, to a ferny old stone bridge over the Laroch River **A**. There is an iron pedestrian bridge as well. Once across, turn up left on a road with pleasant gardens, the United Free church and the local primary school. The road becomes a track at a farm. Note that the fence wires are threaded through holes in 'posts' made of slate. (Local cemeteries even have slate gravestones.)

The route passes a sheep fold and bridges a pleasant stream coming down off the steep hills on the right. Sgorr Dhearg ('red peak') is part of the Beinn a' Bheithir horseshoe walk, a hard, classic circuit as one can imagine from the bold sweeps of mountain skirted by this walk. On the right is an old quarry cutting **B**, but as you climb up a last field you feel quite clear of the industrial past.

Gleann an Fhiodh means 'wooded glen' – ironically, for little original

0	200	400	600	800 METRES	1	
						KILOMETRES
						MILES
0	200	400	600 YARDS	½		

The little harbour at Ballachulish

woodland remains, though at least it is clear of the blanket forestry which approaches it from every side. The name of the Allt Sheileach, which is crossed, means 'willow stream'. After the path follows the River Laroch for a while a cairn is reached ⓒ and here the path forks. The right fork continues up to the Laroch watershed and tree-covered Glen Duror. Take the left fork, which crosses the Laroch.

The path then climbs steeply up to the Mam Uchdaich ('upper hill pass'), the old route through to Appin. The Glen Creran (south) side of the pass is all blanket conifer plantings too, but this high perch, with its marker cairn ⓓ, gives a grand view over to a rough jumble of peaks, all of Corbett or Munro stature. Beinn a' Bheithir (pronounced *ben vair*, and meaning 'peak of thunder') looks quite majestic just to the north-west.

Return by the same route. The view is quite different as it is telescoped by the steep hills. Eilean Munde, visible out in Loch Leven, is an ancient burial ground of the Macdonalds. Some of the clan fled this way after the notorious Massacre of Glencoe in 1692. ●

The Two Passes

Start	Upper Glen Coe
Distance	9 miles (14.5km)
Approximate time	4½ hours
Parking	Small car parks and lay-bys near the Study
Refreshments	None
Ordnance Survey maps	Landranger 41 (Ben Nevis & Fort William) and Outdoor Leisure 38 (Ben Nevis & Glen Coe)

This is probably the finest walk in the Glen Coe area that does not entail climbing a summit. There is still an ascent of 2100ft (640m) to be made, however, and the scenery is on the grand scale. The passes of Lairig Eilde ('pass of the hinds') and Lairig Gartain ('pass of the ticks') form a circular walk right round the elongated peak of the Buachaille Etive Beag ('little Etive shepherd'), and both are classic glaciated U-shaped glens. This is quite a rough walk, and every bit as demanding as a summit. It is recommended only in dry conditions, as several streams are crossed and these can be dangerous in spate.

Park in the first car park or lay-by available above the gorge (the Study) with its waterfall, which is such a feature of motoring up Glen Coe, and then walk up the A82. A large cairn and a SRWS signpost indicate the start of the walk proper **Ⓐ**, though 'Loch Etiveside', given as the destination, is not very accurate. The path angles up to cross the Allt Lairig Eilde (dangerous in spate) **Ⓑ**, follows its north-west bank along under Beinn Fhada for a mile (1.5km), then crosses again for the final pull up to the top of the pass **Ⓒ**, a rise of 800ft (240m) from the road. Stob Dubh (3130ft/958m) rises steeply to the left, highest summit of the Buachaille Etive Beag and a temptingly accessible Munro. Jagged Stob Coire Sgreamhach at 3497ft (1070m) dominates the other side; it is an outlier of Bidean nam Bian, the highest peak in Argyll.

The burn flowing down to Dalness in Glen Etive is also called the Allt Lairig Eilde and the path descends the slopes of its west bank. When a fenced-off area is reached turn down **Ⓓ** to cross the Allt Lairig Eilde, an easy crossing, with views upstream to slabby falls and, below, a tree-filled gorge. Use the path which ascends Stob Dubh direct from Glen Etive to gain some height, and then pick a traverse line across and

Buachaille Etive Mor

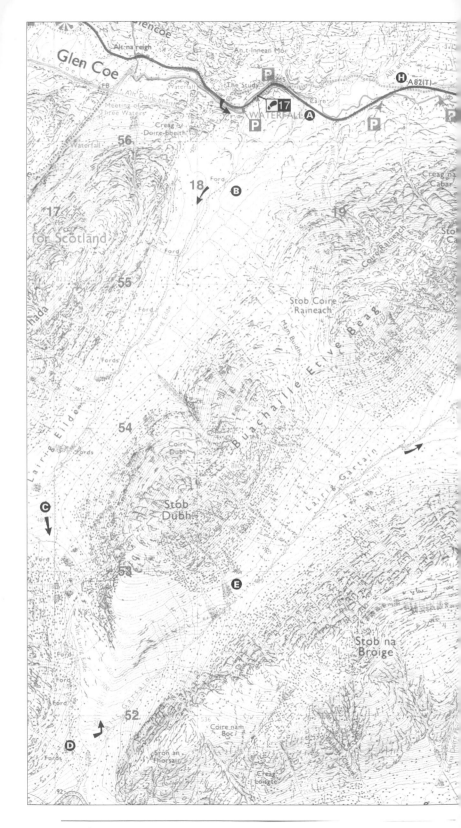

SCALE 1:26316 or about 2½ INCHES to 1 MILE 3.8CM to 1KM

up to the col of the Lairig Gartain **E**, an uphill ascent of about 670ft (200m).

Several cairns lead over the bealach (col), and down the far side the path becomes clearer again as it follows the wide glen of the River Coupall, a rather boggy, heathery route. The path reaches the A82 at the road's highest point (there is a lay-by with an AA telephone at the site of the old quarry) **F**. Just to the west can be seen the legendary Lochan na Fola ('bloody pool'). Cross the A82 to pick up the roughly parallel route of the old road **G**, which offers a gentler, safer, more enjoyable return to the start than following the dangerous main road. The A82 actually cuts through one section near the end **H**. Don't walk along the main road here but still keep to the old road (a gate bars traffic), which curves away and then back to the crags above the gorge of the Study (pronounced *stiddie*, a Scots word for the descriptive Gaelic name meaning 'anvil'). There is a classic view of the Three Sisters of Glen Coe from here – the triple hills on the other side. Cut down to the A82 at the falls; take care and beware of speeding motorists. The waters of the Allt Lairig Eilde pour over a rock wall into the gorge in splendid fashion. A few minutes' (careful) walking up the A82 will lead back to the car.

Dalness, in Glen Etive, is the legendary site of the refuge of Deirdre and Naoise, doomed lovers of the old Fingalian legend common to Ireland and Scotland. In the 1692 Massacre, troops were sent over the Devil's Staircase to seal off upper Glen Coe, but in the winter storms some of the clansmen managed to escape to Glen Etive. Lochan na Fola commemorates a more recent inter-clan fray. ●

0	200	400	600	800 METRES	1
					KILOMETRES
					MILES
0	200	400	600 YARDS	½	

Leum Uilleim

Start	Corrour Station
Distance	8 miles (12.75km)
Approximate time	4 hours
Parking	None (nearest: Tulloch Station)
Refreshments	None
Ordnance Survey maps	Landranger 41 (Ben Nevis & Fort William) and Outdoor Leisure 38 (Ben Nevis & Glen Coe)

At 2972ft (906m) this is an easy Corbett, for the ascent starts at Corrour Station, itself at 1340ft (400m), and the initial-level moor (a corner of the Moor of Rannoch) is crossed on a stalking-path. A graceful hill, it offers extensive views from the top, embracing moors, lochs and innumerable summits. There should be no difficulty fitting the climb in between train times, but double-check these. You can catch the train from any station on the West Highland Line between Bridge of Orchy and Fort William. There is a bunkhouse beside the station and a youth hostel at Loch Ossian 1 mile (1.5km) east, so it would be possible (and you are recommended) to do this walk one day and Walk 14 or Walk 20 the next. Leum Uilleim should not be climbed in the stalking season, mid-August to mid-October, without clearance first being obtained from the estate: telephone (01397) 732200 or ask at the youth hostel, which itself has a telephone.

From a gate at the north end of the station a path heads west towards the northern ridge of the hill. Take this path across the moorland, crossing the Allt Coir' a' Bhric Beag ('stream of the small, speckled corrie') on the way **Ⓐ**. When the path ends continue up to gain the crest of the ridge and follow this upwards, south-west, over Tom an Eoin ('knoll of the bird' – probably eagle) **Ⓑ** to a subsidiary top, Beinn a' Bhric **Ⓒ**, and turn left (east), across a saddle and up the broad ridge to the spacious summit of Leum Uilleim **Ⓓ**. The name means 'William's Leap', but who William was and why he leapt is now forgotten. The hill is an easy Corbett, just as Beinn na Lap, above Loch Ossian, is an easy Munro, because all ascents in this area start with a 1000-ft (300m) height gain.

The Blackwater Reservoir cuts the hill off from the rest of Rannoch Moor. Several lochs were amalgamated when the dam was built. (Walk 21 takes in a visit to the dam.) The building of the railway was another

SCALE 1:27777 or about 2¼ INCHES to 1 MILE 3.6CM to 1KM

Leum Uilleim beyond Corrour Station

great feat. In places it is actually floated on the peat as no bottom could be found. Nearer Rannoch Station is a wood-roofed tunnel built to stop winter snow-drifts. Even on a fine day the scene is stark and desolate, but it is always marvellously evocative.

Return along the same route, or cut the corner across the flank of Beinn a' Bhric **E** to regain the ridge down to the path and Corrour. If you have enough time available, walk along to view Loch Ossian. ●

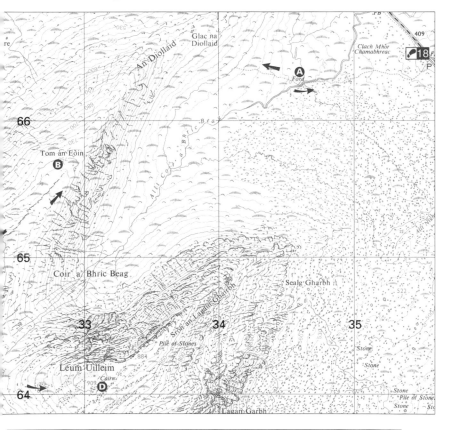

Fraoch Bheinn

Start	West end of Loch Arkaig
Distance	4½ miles (7.25km)
Approximate time	3½ hours
Parking	Roadside at end of public road west of Loch Arkaig
Refreshments	None
Ordnance Survey maps	Landranger 33 (Loch Alsh & Glen Shiel) and Pathfinder 249, NM 89/99 (Glen Dessarry)

The remoteness and wildness of the west is one of Scotland's glories and this is a 'sampler summit' which could well entice the visitor into this area. Standing on the edge of the 'Rough Bounds' and reached by a long, tricky drive, this quite modest hill will probably mean a day's excursion. There is virtually no habitation once the Great Glen is left and the narrow, tortuous road leads through typical western scenery towards the mountains west of Loch Arkaig. The hill itself is fairly craggy but an easy enough climb in good weather. All the hills north of Loch Arkaig form a unit for deer management and are used for stalking. A notice giving details is posted at the Chia-aig Falls car park; or telephone (01738) 628151.

Leave the Great Glen as described in Walk 12 but simply drive on past the Chia-aig Falls to Loch Arkaig which the road follows to its end, an 11-mile (17.5km) convoluted, demanding, narrow road requiring great concentration all the way. The tarmac ends at a turning place where a track heads down to Loch Arkaig and the way on is declared a private road. Park as neatly as possible and walk on along the private road (a right of way for pedestrians). It forks, the left track descending to the smart white house of Strathan, sheep sheds and some derelict buildings. Take the right fork, the Glendessarry track, for a few minutes longer to reach the bridge over the Dearg Allt, where the ascent really commences **Ⓐ**.

The view from here down over the Strathan flats, to the steep, jagged

Fraoch Beinn beyond Strathan

peaks of the Streaps and Sgurr Thuilm, is particularly pleasing. Take the old stalkers' path, to the right, which heads up the east bank of the Dearg Allt (the start of the path is not easy to identify, but walk back from the bridge for about 30 yds (27m). The quality of the path soon improves as it follows the top of the stream bank. On the other side of the Dearg Allt the tracks of ATVs (all-terrain vehicles) have made scars on the hillside.

Follow the path for about ²/₃ mile (1km), topping the first rise of hillside, and cutting in to cross the Dearg Allt **B** at an easier stretch in what is a long, deep-cut gorge. Railings and the ATV path can be seen across and up on the other side. There is a secluded waterfall in the gorge below the railings.

Follow the ATV path for about ten minutes, then simply turn up the pathless hillside – easy grass walking, with the schisty crags aiding rather than hindering the line up on to the south ridge of the hill **C**. The ridge is then followed up to the summit cairn **D**. Fraoch Bheinn, 2808ft (858m) high, may lack a triangulation pillar but has a grand setting nevertheless.

The view looks west to the Rough Bounds of Knoydart, lonely Glen Kingie runs across to the north, and fellow Corbetts stand on either side. Descend the south ridge again **C** and this time follow it all the way down to the

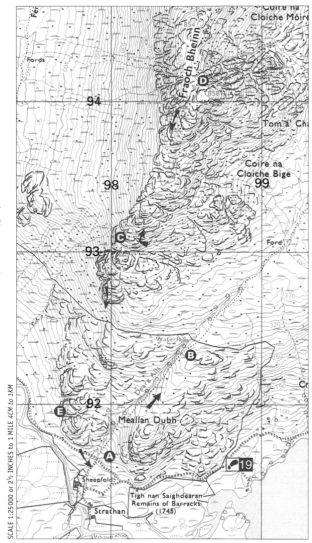

SCALE 1:25000 or 2½ INCHES to 1 MILE 4CM to 1KM

| 0 | 200 | 400 | 600 | 800 METRES | 1 |
| 0 | 200 | 400 | 600 YARDS | ½ | KILOMETRES
MILES |

Glendessarry track. At the last obvious bump **E** it is best to aim down and follow the ATV track. This small bump offers a superb eagle's-eye view up Glen Dessarry with the fang of Sgurr na h-Aide in the distance. Both Glen Dessarry and Glen Pean beyond Strathan have been swamped with conifer plantations.

Allow plenty of time at the end of the walk for the interesting drive back to the Great Glen. ●

Secretive Loch Treig

Start	Corrour Station
Distance	9 miles (14.5km)
Approximate time	4½ hours
Parking	None (nearest: Tulloch Station)
Refreshments	None
Ordnance Survey maps	Landranger 41 (Ben Nevis & Fort William) and Outdoor Leisure 38 (Ben Nevis & Glen Coe)

This walk uses part of the old drovers' route, the 'Road to the Isles' of the song. There is no permanent habitation on the route and it descends to some wild country, so reserve the walk for a day offering good conditions, and carry refreshments.

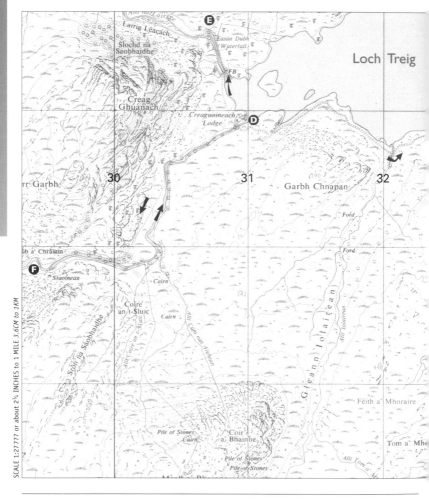

The walk starts at lonely Corrour Station (as do Walks 14 and 18) and descends to the southern end of Loch Treig (used for generating electricity at Fort William aluminium works) before exploring two of the streams which join the loch in this beautiful, remote corner of wildest Lochaber.

Leave the west side of the station by way of a gate leading on to a stalking-path, which soon splits. Turn right to walk along parallel to the railway line. A notice marks the highest point of the line at a height of 1350ft (450m) **Ⓐ**. The path crosses the Allt Coir' a' Bhric Beag and ⅓ mile (0.6km) further on recrosses the same stream, now called the Allt a' Chamabhreac. Railway, path and stream all swing left to avoid the bold prow of hill ahead, Sron na Garbh-bheinne. At the bend in the railway there is a bridge and here you pick up a rough estate track **Ⓑ** which has come from Loch Ossian and leads down to Loch Treig. Turn left just before the loch to cross over the Allt Crunachgan **Ⓒ**.

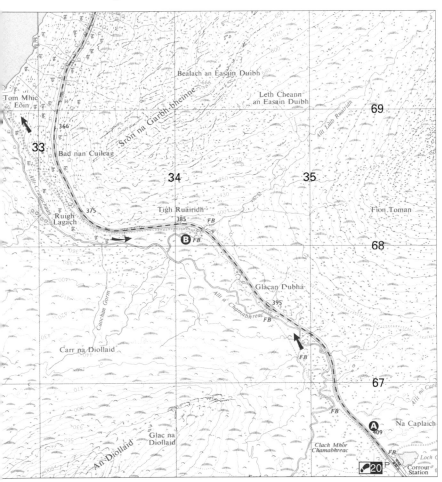

The level of Loch Treig can vary as it is the reservoir supplying water (for hydro power) to the Fort William aluminium works (the water goes by pipe, from the north end of Loch Treig, under Ben Nevis's slopes). From the south shore the hill seen away through the gap of the loch northwards is Beinn Teallach (Walk 22). At Creaguaineach Lodge the estate road comes to an end **D**. Two great routes join here. Westwards, 10 miles (16km) off, lies the Glen Nevis car park (Walk 5) with no habitation on the way; north-west, there are 8 miles (12.75km) of the Lairig Leacach before a house is met at Coirechoille in Strath Spean.

Lairig Leacach means 'slabby pass'; it drains into Loch Treig ('loch of desolation') by the Allt na Lairige, a superb Highland river with many waterfalls, and best in early summer when the new growth of the trees glitters – and cuckoos call incessantly (they are often seen here as well as heard). Take the path northwards from the lodge to a footbridge and up the east bank to the Easan Dubh ('black falls') **E**, then return to the lodge.

This time take the path south-westwards for an even more attractive riverside walk which leads in 1 1/4 miles (2km) to a lonely cottage, Staoineag, now maintained as an open bothy. It lies across on the south side of the Abhainn Rath; the stepping-stones can be underwater in spate conditions. A distant view of Ben Nevis is the reward for reaching this remote spot **F**.

Retrace the route to Corrour Station. Remember there is an uphill finish and allow plenty of time for catching the evening train out, or stay on at the youth hostel by Loch Ossian (or the station bunkhouse) for Walks 14 and 18. Walk 11 (On to Rannoch Moor) starts at Rannoch Station, the next station to the south. ●

Creaguaineach Lodge by Loch Treig

The Heights of Kinlochleven

Start	Kinlochleven
Distance	10 miles (16km). Shorter version 5½ miles (8.75km)
Approximate time	5½ hours (2½ hours for shorter version)
Parking	Centre of Kinlochleven
Refreshments	In Kinlochleven
Ordnance Survey maps	Landranger 41 (Ben Nevis & Fort William) and Outdoor Leisure 38 (Ben Nevis & Glen Coe)

This is quite a long and tiring circular walk but the views must be some of the finest in the country. It is a magnificent and very varied circuit, and must be kept for a clear day. Carry a picnic and make a full day's expedition of the walk, as it deserves. If it is found necessary or desirable to shorten the route, the section heading east to the Blackwater Reservoir may be omitted.

Having parked, find the phone box on the main road (north of the river) and beside it there is a signpost indicating Gray or Grey Mare's Waterfall, depending which side you read! Follow this road, and then a footpath skirts St Paul's episcopal church which is seen ahead. The way to the fall is a well-made path, and climbing up the wooded slope you will hear the roar of the waterfall and, from a viewpoint **A**, see it, deep set in a narrow gorge. (A path leads down to reach the mouth of the gorge if you want a closer look.)

Follow the path on up, passing picnic tables, to come out above the woods, with a power line overhead. Continue heading along a spur of hillside, in a north-easterly direction, then bear left, north, to cross two burns in succession. Beyond the second dip, where two streams meet, the path forks and forks again. Take the right fork both times to head up the hillside by a burn **B**. The path crosses to the other bank then swings off east to climb up to join an estate road where this makes a bend round a jutting crag **C**.

This road comes from Mamore Lodge and is followed almost to Loch Eilde Mor, the next mile (1.5km) giving the classic view back down Loch Leven, the fjord hemmed in by peaks and with the Pap of Glencoe (Walk 15) in the distance. Many would rate it the best view on all these walks.

Loch Leven and the distant Pap of Glencoe

Follow the twisting road over a watershed, and about halfway down from there to Loch Eilde Mor branch off to the right on a poorer path **D**, which leads across to a dam at the start of the Allt na h-Eilde **E**. The waters of Loch Eilde Mor are being taken round and up the next valley to feed the Blackwater Reservoir, whose waters are in turn led along the opposite hillside and then down through massive pipes until they reach the power-house of the aluminium works in Kinlochleven. The process requires large amounts of electricity, hence the siting of this industrial complex, which seems so incongruous, in such a remote corner.

Now follow the pipeline for 1½ miles (2.5km) to the viewpoint spur of Leitir Bo Fionn ('slope of the white cattle').

*A path twists down steeply right **F** to near the meeting of the River Leven and Allt na h-Eilde, the short alternative to the full walk.*

There are another 3½ miles (5.5km) of pipeline to follow to reach the big Blackwater Reservoir dam; the walking can be frustrating in places as there is no real path, and a big bend has to be made round the Allt Coire na Duibhe

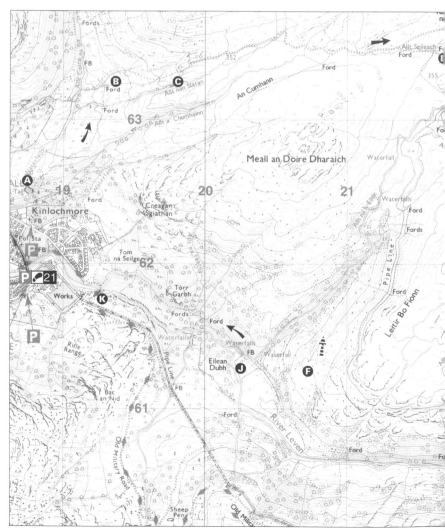

hollow. A good lunch-break by the dam will be appreciated 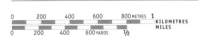.

You cannot cross the top of the dam and it is something of an obstacle course below the dam wall. The curious may want to go over to see the pathetic graves of some of the named, and nameless, navvies who constructed the dam. It was built in 1905–9 to link up several moorland lochs. The Blackwater is now about 8 miles (13km) long. Up to 3000 men slaved to build it, and it was the last massive engineering feat in the Highlands to use navvies. The fictionalised account of its construction is told in MacGill's book and Borthwick also describes some of the story (see the Bibliography on page 95).

The return route is along a path down the north bank of the River Leven, the size of which will depend on how much water is being released from the dam. The path starts by curving *above* the pipeline. but soon cuts down to the Dubh Lochan and thereafter hugs the riverbank. High across the valley can be seen the conduit taking the water from the dam to the penstock and the six huge pipes down to the generators below. In autumn the birch trees here are a brilliant gold. There is a fine fall where the Allt na h-Eilde joins the River Leven and then a last mile through the trees leads back into Kinlochleven. There are many paths, but generally keep to variants near the river which should lead out to a track at a bridge over the River Leven.

This soon swings right as a tarred road, Wade's Road, whose houses have trim gardens. Halfway along, at a West Highland Way sign, turn off for a riverside route to the B863 where it bridges the River Leven. The outflow of water from the power station is a spectacular sight. Pub or chip shop (or both) will be welcome here. Kinlochleven is well geared for walkers, being an overnight stopping place on the West Highland Way. South of the river there is a visitor centre with excellent interpretative displays telling the story of aluminium, and which will helpfully round off what you have seen. Walk 4 offers a similar but shorter walk above Kinlochleven.

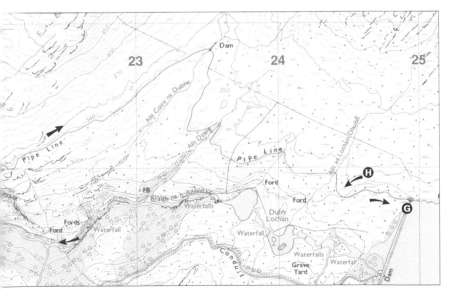

Beinn Teallach

Start	Roughburn
Distance	9 miles (14.5km)
Approximate time	4½ hours
Parking	Roadside at Roughburn; do not block gates
Refreshments	None
Ordnance Survey maps	Landranger 34 (Fort Augustus & Glen Albyn) and Pathfinder 265, NN 28/38 (Lower Glen Roy & Roybridge)

Beinn Teallach, lying on the eastern edge of Brae Lochaber, came to prominence some years ago when new mapping elevated its height to Munro status – 3003ft (915m); only then was its gentle nature recognised, as well as its magnificence as a viewpoint. Massed forestry now cuts it off from the A86 Spean Bridge–Strathspey road, so follow the description of the start carefully. A walk up a valley and down an open ridge makes for a variable expedition, one best made in dry conditions. In the stalking season check access by telephoning (01397) 732217.

The start is at Roughburn, at the west end of Loch Laggan. Park just east of the bridge past the buildings (don't block the gateway), or if this is not practical use the car park overlooking the Laggan dam and walk the ⅓ mile (630m) along to Roughburn.

There is a high stile beside the gate; from there follow the forest track as it wends up through the trees. After

The Laggan dam below Beinn Teallach

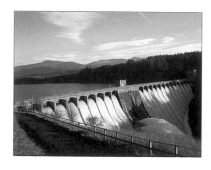

¾ mile (1.25km), as it heads east along the hillside, branch off left **A** on a greener track which heads westwards and down towards the riverside fields. The last 200 yds (182m) are not on constructed track and can be muddy.

Turn upstream (there are gates and a stile through the first small field), following the riverbank to the top fence of the fields. The fence crosses the river and, after going through the gate, the walker follows suit, picking up a good path on the opposite bank **B**. There is no bridge; in spate the Allt a' Chaorainn may not be passable and the rough east bank would have to be followed as far as necessary.

The footpath is followed for 2½ miles (4km) up to the col of Tom

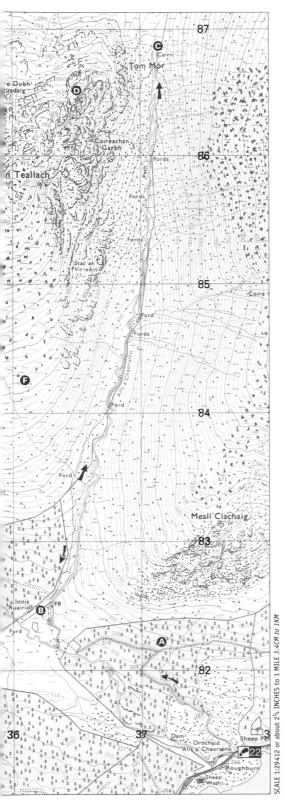

SCALE 1:29412 or about 2⅛ INCHES to 1 MILE 3.4CM to 1KM

Mor where there is a finger of cairn **C**. The east face of Beinn Teallach (pronounced *challach* – the name means 'hill of the forge') is called Coireachan Garbh. *Garbh* means 'rough', and the aptness of the name is evident. Swing west beyond the cairn to climb the north-east ridge above the crags **D**, on rough but easy enough ground, to the summit **E**. The Highland hills are basically an eroded plateau and the view north from the summit shows this clearly. The huge Glen Spean trench cuts across south of this hill, with a long view down Loch Treig.

The descent is made by heading south and then more to the south-east, down an even slope of gentle nature **F** which the young will delight to take at a gallop. Aim for the apex of the plantation and rejoin the path to cross the Allt a' Chaorainn again **B** and return by the forest tracks to Roughburn.

Before leaving, have a look at the Laggan dam. One of the earliest (pre-war) hydro schemes, its water catchment feeds Loch Treig from here, and thence goes via a tunnel to the aluminium works at Fort William. ●

Beinn Dòrain

Start	Bridge of Orchy
Distance	5½ miles (8.75km)
Approximate time	4½ hours
Parking	Station car park at Bridge of Orchy
Refreshments	Hotel, Bridge of Orchy
Ordnance Survey maps	Landranger 50 (Glen Orchy) and Outdoor Leisure 38 (Ben Nevis & Glen Coe)

As you head north on the A82, the top of the pass above Tyndrum brings a soaring cone of hill into view. This is Beinn Dòrain, pronounced doorun. *The ascent, fortunately, is made from the other side and, while steep, presents no real difficulty if the described route is adhered to.* In winter it is more demanding, best left to those with winter skills – the same caution also applies to Walks 24–28.

Bridge of Orchy on the A82 is a popular walkers' base, lying as it does on the West Highland Way and surrounded by a good selection of high peaks. Start from the station car park, heading through under the West Highland Line pedestrian underpass to gain the path up the hillside beside the Allt Coire an Dothaidh **Ⓐ**. Follow this up into Coire an Dothaidh where it rather peters out. Head for the obvious col but before

reaching it swing right **Ⓑ** below the crags on the col and ascend, steeply, still below the crags, to come out on to a flatter area marked by a lochan **Ⓒ**.

Beyond the lochan head south and the well-defined ridge (with some minor crags to skirt) will eventually lead to the summit. There is a false summit first with a cairn **Ⓓ**, the real summit lying about 350 yds (320km) beyond. There is no doubt when you are at the summit cairn itself **Ⓔ**.

Beinn Dòrain is one of a cluster of five Munros which the energetic sometimes walk in a single outing. The summit panorama shows a vast array of lumpy hills, but among this Perthshire-Argyll mix there are some giants which stand out: Ben More and Stobinian, which dominate Crianlarich, Ben Lui near

Beinn Dòrain from the Tyndrum road

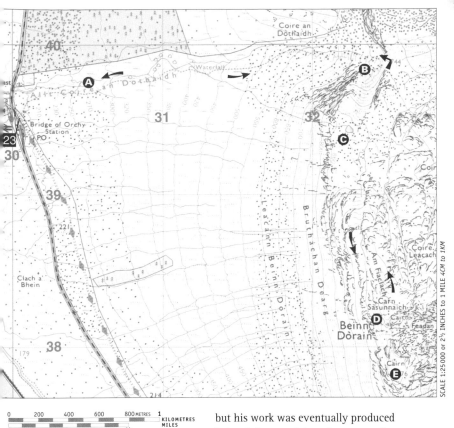

SCALE 1:25000 or 2½ INCHES to 1 MILE 4CM to 1KM

0 200 400 600 800 METRES 1
KILOMETRES
MILES
0 200 400 600 YARDS ½

Tyndrum, Cruachan above Loch Awe, and Stob Ghabhar. Beinn Dòrain, at 3530ft (1076m), is a worthy ascent. Return by the same route used on the way out. Refreshments are available at the hotel in Bridge of Orchy.

Beinn Dòrain is one of those peaks which have a close historical association with one man. Duncan Ban MacIntyre was a great 18th-century Gaelic poet. Born in the shadow of Stob Ghabhar (Walk 25) he spent many years as a keeper on Beinn Dòrain and at Dalness in Glen Etive (Walk 17). Like many keepers he was a gifted naturalist, but he was also a poet and poured out his feelings in notable poems, the most famous being 'In Praise of Beinn Dòrain' (*Moladh Beinn Dobhrain*). Duncan Ban, 'Fair Duncan of the Songs', was actually illiterate,

but his work was eventually produced in book form and there is a story of a 'reading' he gave in Edinburgh (where he served in the city guard) at which he held the book upside down, quite oblivious of the fact.

Beinn Dòrain's name has two possible origins. It could be 'hill of the streams', which would be appropriate, for its slopes are seamed with obvious watercourses, or it could be 'hill of the otter', a common enough derivation. Otters are still seen in the Highlands and their Gaelic name is *dobhar-chu*, 'water dog'. Whether or not the hill is named after the otter, it is certainly well known for frogs, and the contemporary poet Norman MacCaig has written several poems celebrating the fact. There is some mystery as to why frogs (and adders) are found on only certain Highland hills and not all of them. There must be some reason for their selectiveness!   ●

Ben Tee

Start	Laggan Locks
Distance	8½ miles (13.5km)
Approximate time	5 hours
Parking	Laggan Locks
Refreshments	Tearoom, Laggan Locks
Ordnance Survey maps	Landranger 34 (Fort Augustus & Glen Albyn) and Pathfinder 251, NN 29/39 (Laggan, Highland)

This isolated hill, 2957ft (901m) high, is one of the finest viewpoints in Scotland, offering a huge panoramic sweep over the West Highlands. The peak dominates Glen Garry and the climb from the Great Glen gives a variety of river, wood, moor and mountain landscape that is typical of the west. The ascent should not be underestimated: the terrain is rough throughout, and standard mountain skills are needed – in poor weather good map and compass work is demanded. *The Kilfinnan Falls are not an easy alternative. One mile (1.5km) northwards along the A82 is Loch Lochy youth hostel.*

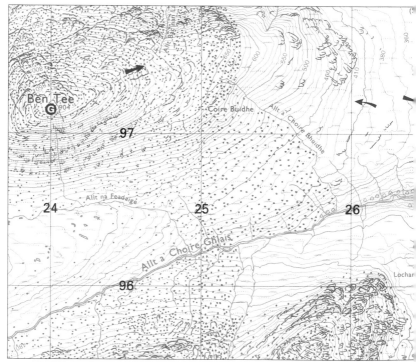

Kilfinnan is a sheep farm so dogs are not welcome. *The route of this walk is on Forestry Commission land and stalking does not start till the second week of September, but you can check by telephoning the forest office at Torlundy on (01397) 702184.*

The walk starts at Laggan Locks on the Caledonian Canal, where the canal enters the north end of Loch Lochy. Telford's superb creation reaches its highest point at the locks, and the tearoom has a display of photographs of the canal in bygone days. (Walk 8 follows the canal, from the south end of Loch Lochy.) The locks are on the site of a bloody clan fight of 1544 when only 12 men survived out of 900. A plaque explains why it was called the Battle of the Shirts.

The locks and tearoom are signposted from the A82. Park in the picnic parking site off the approach road and not at the locks. Cross the canal and walk round the head of Loch Lochy, passing some chalets and joining a minor road that leads along to the sheep farm of Kilfinnan. The road continues as a forestry road, but turn off up the north bank of the Kilfinnan Burn . Note the huge boulders carried down by recent spates.

The Kilfinnan Burn is set in a deep cleft with steep flanks, and the approach to the falls requires a great deal of confidence in walking on steep, sometimes exposed slopes. Take an initial path up along the north bank, keeping generally at the top of the treeline in the gorge where there are

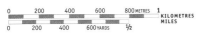

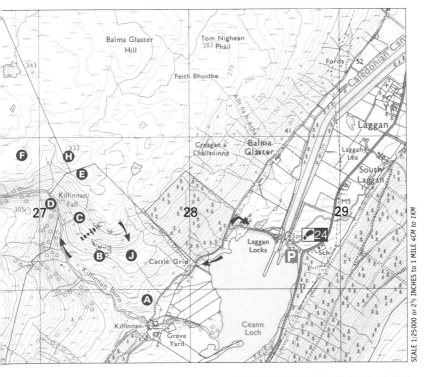

The approach to Ben Tee: Kilfinnan from Laggan Locks

sheep trails to follow **B**. When the falls are visible through the trees scramble up the steep slope for 50ft (15m) to obtain an unobstructed view – and decide there about going any closer **C**.

Whatever you decide to do, the steep banking has to be toiled up, as the falls block progress other than via the top of the bank. The narrow path onwards can be intimidating and dangerous in wet conditions but leads very near to the falls **D**, giving a superb view of the mighty plunge of water falling into a black pool. From there there is a very strenuous haul up to the top of the bank, as indeed there is from the more distant viewing spot, the slopes being steep heather. Eventually a path wandering along near the crest of the bank is reached, and this leads to a meeting of fences and a stile not far upstream from the level of the falls **E**. (The fence can be seen earlier on when you look up past the falls.)

The stile over the deer fence leads on to the moorland sprawl, beyond which rises the shapely peak of Ben Tee. The path can be seen continuing along the top of the gorge and can be taken for another five minutes. Then leave the path **F** to make a beeline for Ben Tee, a reasonably uncomplicated hill rising as it does in steady fashion to the final stony cone **G**: a tiny top with an almighty view to the west, and a bird's-eye view up the Great Glen, too – one of the best summit views in Scotland, typical of a Corbett. The two neighbouring Munros to the south-west by no means dominate Ben Tee.

Follow the route of the ascent back to the stile over the deer fence **E**. Note that there is another stile at a gate just 220 yds (0.25km) along the fence **H**, which could be confusing in mist. The fence itself is a useful guide if a mist descends since, wherever met, if it is followed to the right the stile will be reached, and the path home from there is clear enough.

The path follows the high ground of the bank above the gorge as long as possible, so there is no view of the falls to be had, but from the last spur **J** there is a dramatic downward view to Laggan Locks and the loch itself. The path takes the obvious route down the spur back to Kilfinnan; if you should lose it a bit on steeper sections it can usually be spotted below and rejoined. It was probably only a sheep track originally but is now being tramped by walkers heading for Ben Tee. The old ruined church and burial ground are seen beside the farm, and boats may be seen approaching the locks – apparently a landscape in miniature. ●

Stob Ghabhar

Start	Victoria Bridge
Distance	9½ miles (15.25km)
Approximate time	6 hours
Parking	Off-road, Victoria Bridge
Refreshments	Nearest at hotel, Bridge of Orchy
Ordnance Survey maps	Landranger 50 (Glen Orchy) and Outdoor Leisure 38 (Ben Nevis & Glen Coe)

This peak represents another step up the ladder from the standard of any walk already described. It is a big, sculpted, rocky mass which needs to be treated with caution, even in the perfect conditions it deserves for an ascent. It occupies a historic place in mountaineering history: several winter climbs were made last century on the crags and corries flanking the ridges up which walkers, perforce, must go. Potential navigation difficulties make a clear day a priority. In winter, keep off. Note that in the stalking season the round trip is not possible, the route back down simply retracing that of the ascent.

Turn west off the A82 at Bridge of Orchy, cross the old military bridge and go on by the fine woods and Loch Tulla to the road-end at Victoria Bridge/ Forest Lodge. Park just before the bridge. From the Forest Lodge road-end (turning only) an estate road heads west, parallel to the Abhainn Shira. At the small green tin hut turn right Ⓐ on to a footpath up the Allt Toaig. (The hut is a university climbing hut and reputedly once slept 35. Originally it was a school.)

If the Allt Toaig is in spate go up its west bank via the footbridge rather than risk crossing from the path later on.

The path runs for about 1½ miles (2.5km) up into Coire Toaig but should be abandoned after about a mile (1.5km), where the stream coming down from Coire na Muic ('pig corrie') joins the Allt Toaig Ⓑ. After crossing these streams head west, then north-west for the broad south ridge of Stob Ghabhar, picking a line round some crags, scree and generally rough ground. There is a

Stob Ghabhar from Stob a' Choire Odhair

levelling-off on the ridge **C** then a steep pull up to a bump on the final corrie-bitten arc, with the summit 350 yds (320m) to the north-west **D**. The big feature of the summit area is the north-east corrie, which has been carved out by glaciation. At 3575ft (1090m) Stob Ghabhar is certainly big. After all your exertions you may feel the name – 'hill of the goat' – is appropriate; it is one of the commonest hill names, and pronounced *gowar*.

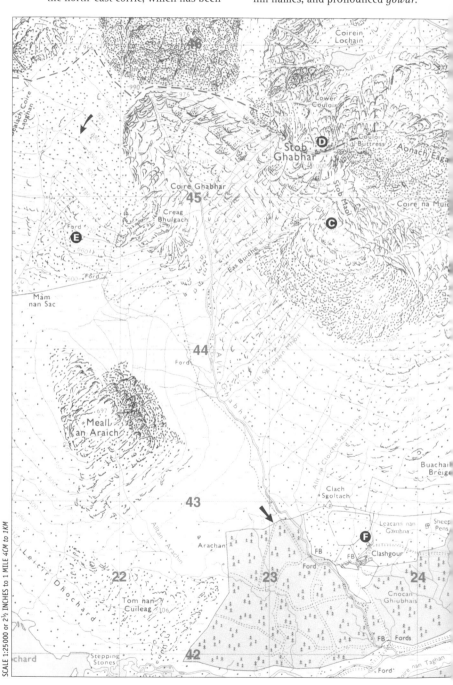

SCALE 1:25000 or 2½ INCHES to 1 MILE *4CM to 1KM*

Coire Ghabhar to the west is also a fine corrie, and a pleasant way down (outside the stalking season) is to circle round the top of it and pick up the stalking-path shown near Màm nan Sac **E**. Follow this down the Allt Ghabhar to Clashgour **F** from where a mile of estate road through a plantation leads back to the hut **A** where the ascent began. In the stalking season descend by the route used for the ascent rather than by Coire Ghabhar.

The great poet of Beinn Dòrain (Walk 23), Duncan Ban MacIntyre, was born near Loch Tulla. A rough track leads west from the road 300 yds (273m) south of Victoria Bridge and after ¹/₂ mile (800m) passes a monument which marks the poet's birthplace. As is so often the case, there is nothing much to show that people once lived here. Both up Glen Fuar, where the track ends, and in Doire Darach, the wood to the south of Loch Tulla as you drive out to Bridge of Orchy, there are good examples (even if they are sad remnants) of the woodland that once covered much of Scotland. Another fine remnant of the Wood of Caledon is Cranach Wood, which the train passes through if you take the line to the Rannoch and Corrour Station walks from Bridge of Orchy. The wood is about 6 miles (9.5km) north-east of Bridge of Orchy. ●

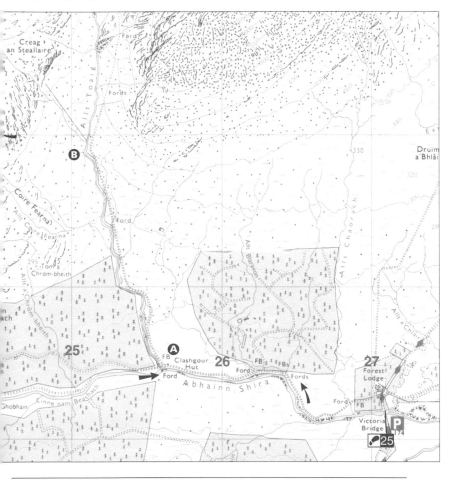

Stob Bàn

Start	Polldubh, Glen Nevis
Distance	6½ miles (10.5km)
Approximate time	5½ hours
Parking	Car park, Polldubh
Refreshments	None
Ordnance Survey maps	Landranger 41 (Ben Nevis & Fort William), Outdoor Leisure 38 (Ben Nevis & Glen Coe)

The Mamore Forest is one of the finest hill ranges in the country, a sea of summits, eleven of them of Munro stature, all highly regarded, all demanding. Stob Bàn means 'white peak': its final rocks are quartzite. The ascent is by an old stalkers' path so is not too difficult technically, but the scale and the height to be climbed render it a strenuous walk. The final pull involves plenty of loose rock and scree. A clear day is recommended and the peak is best climbed before the stalking season.

The start is up Glen Nevis, a pleasant drive in itself (Walk 5 lies at the head of the glen); park below the Polldubh Crags just after the road swings across the River Nevis. Below the bridge are the Lower Falls, a short plunge between red rocks. Cross the bridge to the south and ignore the riverbank gate and stile, but take the stile immediately after (where a notice says sheep graze here).

Stob Bàn

The route curves round and steadily climbs up beside the Allt Coire a' Mhusgain. After a mile (1.5km) the glen draws in and the path turns up left to gain height in a series of zigzags **Ⓐ**. Care is needed not to overshoot this sudden change of direction – so many have done so that there is a tempting, but false, path ahead. The view back from this point is down the full length of lower Glen Nevis. Stob Bàn, just south-west, presents a rather dramatic aspect at this stage, appearing a great jagged rock peak.

The path now makes a traverse, swings across the main burn of the glen, and winds up to the saddle between Stob Bàn (west) and Sgorr an Iubhair (east). The ascent path meets one running along the saddle **Ⓑ**; turn right on to this (briefly,

SCALE 1:25000 or 2½ INCHES to 1 MILE 4CM to 1 KM

0	200	400	600	800 METRES	1
					KILOMETRES
					MILES
0	200	400	600 YARDS	½	

for it turns down left) and keep ahead **C** to tackle the now rather less formidable-looking final upthrust of Stob Bàn. There is a lot of loose, sharp, quartzite rock and scree, which makes the ascent into a bit of a scramble. The 3274ft (999m) summit **D** offers a view over much of the country covered by this book. The Mamores surge away to the east, and northwards lies the bulk of Ben Nevis (see Walk 28).

Tucked in below the saddle leading to Sgorr an Iubhair (pronounced *you-ar*) can be seen a tiny lochan, and this is an excellent spot for a picnic or even a swim on a hot day **E**. Lochan Coire nam Miseach ('the kids corrie pool') is always marvellously clear and cool.

Eventually reverse the route back down to Polldubh in Glen Nevis.

The crags above the car park are a favourite area for rock-climbing so you may well see people trying their skills on them.

Ben Starav

Start	Coileitir road-end, Glen Etive
Distance	7½ miles (12km)
Approximate time	5½–6 hours
Parking	Off-road near start in Glen Etive
Parking	Off-road near start
Refreshments	None
Ordnance Survey maps	Landranger 50 (Glen Orchy) and Outdoor Leisure 38 (Ben Nevis & Glen Coe)

This mighty hill offers the toughest walk in this book's selection – only Ben Nevis is potentially more demanding. The day starts at sea-level to climb 3541ft (1078m) by unrelenting ridges which are rocky and narrow near the summit. Starav's splendid isolation can cause rapid changes of weather on top. These potential difficulties and dangers are precisely why the hill is so highly regarded, and it is a good representative of the bigger, harder Munros not otherwise covered in this book. If Ben Starav 'goes' comfortably you can then think of the Buachaille, Bidean, Carn Mor Dearg and the Aonachs. The hill should be avoided in the stalking season; avoid disturbing sheep in spring. In winter it is best left for the experienced mountaineer.

Ben Starav is a granite hill and a great deal of rock breaks through to the surface. As it is one of the highest peaks the glaciers have bitten out fine corries, with well-defined ridges between. The rivers have cut deep and there are dozens of falls, bare slabs and golden pools. Set off early to use the coolest part of the day for the long upward toil – and to find the best parking places.

After parking take the private track over the River Etive to the cottage of Coileitir and then the path on down the glen. The Allt Mheuran is bridged **A** and, once across, turn left on the path leading high into the heart of the hill. (A short-cut path **B** turns off just past

Coileitir to slant up to the Allt Mheuran, which is easily crossed unless there has been a great deal of rain.)

The path wends up west of the Allt Mheuran and, just before the side-stream of the Allt nam Meirleach is reached, it forks **C**. One branch heads left across the stream to continue up the Allt Mheuran; the other, which is followed, keeps above a shallow gorge on up the Allt nam Meirleach valley, into the very heart of Ben Starav. Just before the fork in the paths (which is not too clear) there is a good view, up left, of the Eas nam Meirleach

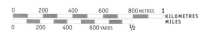

('Robbers' Waterfall') which seems to have been misnamed (one would expect the Meirleach Falls to be on the Meirleach stream!). Where the stream draining Coire an Fhir Leith tumbles into the Meirleach there is a fine but obscured fall which also claims to be the Robbers' Fall **D**. All the falls are annoyingly difficult to see from close at hand. No matter, the scenery is on a grand scale.

The path continues well up the Allt nam Meirleach. Many streams come down the upper slopes, Glas Bheinn Mhór is the dominant hill on the left, and the lowest dip on the skyline is your destination – not nearly as steep as a frontal view suggests. If you follow up the burn (the path ends just across it) there is a tiny pool, Lochan Gaineamhaich ('pool of the stirk', ie. bullock), where a pause may be

Ben Starav viewed down Glen Etive

welcome **E**. Make the most of it: the bare granite above offers no water sources for further refreshment.

From the col **F** the ridge is followed westwards to the summit. It is well defined but it changes direction several times over prows or minor tops before reaching the last, tent-like, near-level ridge. The highest point lies at the far end, a last rocky highway with the sharp edge of the summit corrie on the right. The sight of the triangulation pillar **G** will be greeted with feelings of both pride and relief. The upper reaches are very rough and/or bouldery and edged with impressive granite cliffs – expert navigation is required if conditions are cloudy.

There is an eagle's-eye view over Loch Etive, the setting of the legend of Deirdre of the Sorrows and unhappy Naoise. Bidean nam Bian, highest peak in Argyll, is the only near hill that can compete with Ben Starav. To the south lie the peaks of Cruachan Ben, with several 'horns'. Oddly, the meaning of Ben Starav's name is no longer known.

The descent is relatively simple: just follow down the well-defined north-north-east ridge **H**. There are few places in Britain where you will descend 3100ft (1000m) in just 2 miles (3.25km), so the hard work continues. Traces of path are noticed once the rocky heights are left behind. Maybe effort can be rewarded by a traditional plunge into one of the golden pools on the Allt Mheuran before the right turn back to Coileitir. ●

Preambule...

Ben Nevis

Start	Glen Nevis Youth Hostel, Visitor Centre or Achintee
Distance	8 miles (12.75km)
Approximate time	6–7 hours
Parking	Car parks at Glen Nevis Youth Hostel, Visitor Centre or Achintee
Refreshments	Glen Nevis or Fort William
Ordnance Survey maps	Landranger 41 (Ben Nevis & Fort William), Outdoor Leisure 38 (Ben Nevis & Glen Coe)

Ben Nevis, at 4418ft (1344m), is Britain's highest summit and as such has a lure beyond that of any other. Unfortunately, many visitors with no real mountain experience casually decide to go and climb it, and every year there are casualties – and sometimes fatalities – as a result. Climbing Ben Nevis is a serious undertaking, which is why it is Walk 28. Walks 21 to 27 may offer untracked sections and be technically more difficult, but people going on these hills are likely to be better prepared. The Ben, as a one-off climb, has greater potential for disaster.

The summit lies on the edge of the biggest cliffs of any British hill, so navigation has to be confident and accurate. A sunny day at Fort William can still see the top of Ben Nevis in cloud or storm, and such weather can also sweep in far more quickly than an ascent can be made. The average mean temperature is just below freezing. It can snow on any day of the year. On nine days out of ten the top stays in cloud. These are warning statistics. In winter the ascent should only be tackled by experienced mountaineers, able to navigate in blinding storms, and technically skilled in using ice-axe and crampons. In any case, competent compass work is required.

Boots are essential, and do carry plenty of spare clothing and plenty of refreshments. Take it slowly and steadily. You will actually be surprised how easy the climb proves: there is a path all the way! Alas, the path, even in summer, may be covered in snow up on the summit plateau and navigation must be by map and compass if it is cloudy (footprints in the snow can be going anywhere). If you become at all worried, turn down while still able to do so; it is better to come again than to become one of the accident statistics. Don't hesitate to ask advice locally, in the youth hostel, camp site, Nevisport or tourist office. If you are using this book regularly, you will get far more out of the climb by making this one of the last walks to be tackled. With experience, on a clear day, it *is* easy, and marvellously satisfying.

The climb is a long, hard grind on rough and/or loose surfaces and snow lingers long on the summit plateau. Back down you will find it hard to believe that the Ben Nevis Race record time, for Fort William to the top and back, stands at under 1 ^{1}/$_2$ hours!

There are three regularly used starting points: the youth hostel in Glen Nevis or the nearby camp site – a footbridge from the hostel leads to a steep path up to join the Tourist Track; a car park at the Visitor Centre lower down the glen, where a footbridge crosses to a path which leads up to Achintee, the start of the Tourist Track; Achintee itself, where there is a bunk-house and other accommodation (signposted, off A82, on leaving Fort William). The second is the best starting point for the car-driver, as parking at the other places is limited.

From Achintee the Tourist Track climbs steadily up across the hillside on a long rising traverse. Originally built as a pony path for the Victorian summit observatory and hotel, the path is very stony and rough, but try to walk up slowly and steadily, and enjoy pauses. Resist the temptation of 'short cuts'. All the streams are bridged. There are good views up the glen, and Stob Bàn (Walk 26) looks impressive from the path.

The path puts in a couple of elbow bends **A** and, after these zigzags, climbs up at a steeper angle, from the Glen Nevis flank into the hollow of the Red Burn. When the back wall of this is reached the proper path elbows left **B** to turn up on to the broad saddle holding Lochan Meall an t-Suidhe (Half Way Loch). Don't take the worn short cut straight up the hillside.

There is a junction with a path bearing off left to traverse above the loch and down to the Allt a' Mhuilinn glen and the big Nevis cliffs, a route which is best left to the experts. The Tourist Track soon swings sharply right **C** and rises steadily up to the Red Burn **D**. An old pony shelter here was known as the Half Way Hut and, with the more dangerous half lying ahead, this is the place to turn back if conditions or feelings are not encouraging. After this you are really committed to the grand adventure.

Ahead lies 1000ft (300m) of stone and scree with the path gaining height in seemingly endless zigzags **E**. Keep to the path. When the angle relents you are on the summit plateau **F**, a huge, featureless area of boulders (or snow) at varying levels, across which one tramps for ^{1}/$_2$ mile (800m) to gain the summit. In places the path is very close to the

SCALE 1:26316 or about 2½ INCHES to 1 MILE 3.8CM to 1KM

cliffs, and if there is snow on the ground and bright mist, the edge can be almost impossible to see.

There is no mistaking the summit **G**. There is a triangulation pillar on a cairn, the remains of the observatory buildings with a tiny emergency shelter on top, numerous unnecessary cairns, and a deal of litter. But what a place to be. Half of Scotland seems to be in view. There will almost certainly be other people about, so you can share the reward of being highest in Britain for a few moments.

Ben Nevis's real fame is as a climbers' hill and as such it is world famous. A glance down the cliffs will demonstrate why. A vast array of precipices, ridges and gullies falls 2000ft (600m) to the Allt a' Mhuilinn valley. The observatory operated from 1883 to 1904 (see the bibliography on page 95; Kilgour's *Twenty Years on Ben Nevis*, etc). There is no clear indication of the meaning of the name Nevis, which could have its roots in the Gaelic words meaning both 'heaven' and 'hell'.

The magnificent cliffs of Ben Nevis – Britain's highest peak

The initial progress downwards may call for taking, and following, a careful compass bearing. The summit plateau can be a highly confusing place, and more people go astray leaving it for the descent than in any other way.

The upward route is reversed in full, a three-hour descent for most, with care still needed at every step. There will be a grand feeling of achievement when the ascent – and descent – of Britain's highest hill is over, a fitting climax to walking in the Lochaber area. ●

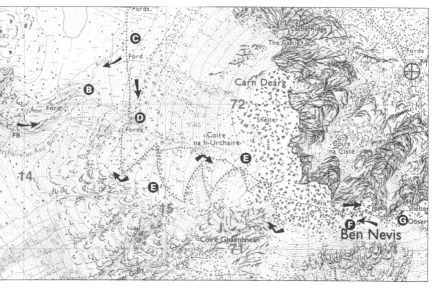

Further Information

The law and tradition as they affect walking in Scotland

Walkers following the routes given in this book should not run into problems, but it is as well to know something about the law as it affects access, and also something of the traditions which can sometimes be quite different in Scotland from elsewhere in Britain. Most of this is common sense, observing the country code and having consideration for other people and their activities which, after all, may be their livelihood.

It is often said that there is no law of trespass in Scotland. In fact there is, but the trespass itself is not usually a criminal offence. You can be asked to leave any property, and technically 'reasonable force' may be used to obtain your compliance – though the term is not defined! You can be charged with causing damage due to the trespass, but this would be hard to establish if you were just walking on open, wild, hilly country where, whatever the law, in practice there has been a long tradition of free access for recreational walking – something both the Scottish Landowners' Federation and the Mountaineering Council of Scotland do not want to see changed.

There are certain restrictions. Walkers should obey the country code and seasonal restrictions arising from lambing or stalking. Where there is any likelihood of such restrictions this is mentioned in the text and visitors are asked to comply. When camping, use a campsite. Camp fires should not be lit; they are a danger to moorland and forest, and really not necessary as lightweight and efficient stoves are now available.

Many of the walks in this book are on rights of way. The watchdog on rights of way in Scotland is the Scottish Rights of Way Society (SRWS), who maintain details on all established cases and will, if need be, contest attempted closures. They produce a booklet on the Scottish legal

The Lairig Gartain from Glen Etive

position (Rights of Way, A Guide to the Law in Scotland, 1991), and their green signposts are a familiar sight by many footpaths and tracks, indicating the lines of historic routes.

In Scotland rights of way are not marked on Ordnance Survey maps as is the case south of the border. It was not felt necessary to show these as such on the maps – a further reflection of the freedom to roam that is enjoyed in Scotland. So a path on a map is no indication of a right of way, and many paths and tracks of great use to walkers were built by estates as stalking paths or for private access. While you may traverse such paths, taking due care to avoid damage to property and the natural environment, you should obey restricted access notices and leave if asked to do so.

The only established rights of way are those where a court case has resulted in a legal judgment, but there are thousands of other 'claimed' rights of way. Local planning authorities have a duty to protect rights of way – this is no easy task with only limited resources. Many attempts at closing claimed rights of way have been successfully contested in the courts by the Scottish Rights of Way Society and local authorities.

A dog on a lead or under control may also be taken on a right of way. There is little chance of meeting a free-range solitary bull on any of the walks. Any herds seen are not likely to be dairy cattle, but all cows can be inquisitive and may approach walkers, especially if they have a dog. Dogs running around among stock may be shot on the spot; this is not draconian legislation but a desperate attempt to stop sheep and lambs being harmed, driven to panic or lost, sometimes with fatal results. Any practical points or restrictions applicable will be made in the text of each walk. If there is no comment it can be assumed that the route carries no real restrictions.

Scotland in fact likes to keep everything as natural as possible, so, for instance, waymarking is kept to a minimum (the Scottish Rights of Way Society signposts and Forest Walk markers are in unobtrusive colours). In Scotland people are asked to 'walk softly in the wilderness, to take nothing except photographs, and leave nothing except footprints' – which is better than any law.

 ### Scotland's Hills and Mountains: a Concordat on Access

This remarkable agreement was published early in 1996 and is likely to have considerable influence on walkers' rights in Scotland in the future. The signatories include organisations which have formerly been at odds - the Scottish Landowners' Federation and the Ramblers' Association, for example. However they joined with others to make the Access Forum (a full list of signatories is detailed below). The RSPB and the National Trust for Scotland did not sign the Concordat initially but it is hoped that they will support its principles.

The signatories of the Concordat are:

Association of Deer Management Groups
Convention of Scottish Local Authorities
Mountaineering Council of Scotland
National Farmers' Union of Scotland
Ramblers' Association Scotland
Scottish Countryside Activities Council
Scottish Landowners' Federation
Scottish Natural Heritage
Scottish Sports Association
Scottish Sports Council

They agreed that the basis of access to the hills for the purposes of informal recreation should be:

Freedom of access exercised with responsibility and subject to reasonable constraints for management and conservation purposes.
Acceptance by visitors of the needs of land management, and understanding of how this sustains the livelihood, culture and community interests of those who live and work in the hills.

Further Information

Acceptance by land managers of the public's expectation of having access to the hills.

Acknowledgment of a common interest in the natural beauty and special qualities of Scotland's hills, and the need to work together for their protection and enhancement.

The Forum point out that the success of the Concordat will depend on all who manage or visit the hills acting on these four principles. In addition, the parties to the Concordat will promote good practice in the form of:

Courtesy and consideration at a personal level.

 ## Glossary of Gaelic Names

Most of the place-names in this region are Gaelic in origin, and this list gives some of the more common elements, which will allow readers to understand otherwise meaningless words and appreciate the relationship between place-names and landscape features. Place-names often have variant spellings, and the more common of these are given here.

aber	mouth of loch, river	eilidh	hind
abhainn	river	eòin, eun	bird
allt	stream	fionn	white
auch, ach	field	fraoch	heather
bal, bail, baile	town, homestead	gabhar, ghabhar,	
bàn	white, fair, pale	gobhar	goat
bealach	hill pass	garbh	rough
beg, beag	small	geal	white
ben, beinn	hill	ghlas, glas	grey
bhuidhe	yellow	gleann, glen	narrow, valley
blar	plain	gorm	blue, green
brae, braigh	upper slope,	inbhir, inver	confluence
	steepening	inch, inis, innis	island, meadow by
breac	speckled		river
cairn	pile of stones, often	lag, laggan	hollow
	marking a summit	làrach	old site
cam	crooked	làirig	pass
càrn	cairn, cairn-shaped	leac	slab
	hill	liath	grey
caol, kyle	strait	loch	lake
ceann, ken, kin	head	lochan	small loch
cil, kil	church, cell	màm	pass, rise
clach	stone	maol	bald-shaped top
clachan	small village	monadh	upland, moor
cnoc	hill, knoll, knock	mór, mor(e)	big
coille, killie	wood	odhar, odhair	dun-coloured
corrie, coire,		rhu, rubha	point
choire	mountain hollow	ruadh	red, brown
craig, creag	cliff, crag	sgòr, sgòrr,	
crannog,		sgùrr	pointed
crannag	man-made island	sron	nose
dàl, dail	field, flat	stob	pointed
damh	stag	strath	valley (broader than
dearg	red		glen)
druim, drum	long ridge	tarsuinn	traverse, across
dubh, dhu	black, dark	tom	hillock (rounded)
dùn	hill fort	tòrr	hillock (more rugged)
eas	waterfall	tulloch, tulach	knoll
eilean	island	uisge	water, river

A welcome to visitors.

Making advice readily available on the ground or in advance.

Better information about the uplands and hill land uses through environmental education.

Respect by visitors for the welfare needs of livestock and wildlife.

Adherence to relevant codes and standards of good practice by visitors and land managers alike.

Any local restrictions on access should be essential for the needs of management, should be fully explained, and be for the minimum period and area required.

Queries should be addressed to: Access Forum Secretariat, c/o Recreation and Access Branch, Scottish Natural Heritage, 2 Anderson Place, Edinburgh EH6 5NP.

 ## Safety on the Hills

The Highland hills and lower but remote areas call for care and respect. The idyllic landscape of the tourist brochures can change rapidly into a world of gales, rain and mist, potentially lethal for those ill-equipped or lacking the right navigational skills. The Scottish hills in winter can be arctic in their severity, and even in the height of summer, snow can lash the summits. It is essential that the walker is aware of these hazards, which are discussed in greater detail in the introduction to this book.

At the very least carry adequate wind- and waterproof outer garments, food and drink to spare, a basic first-aid kit, whistle, map and compass – and know how to use them. Wear boots. Plan within your capabilities. If going alone ensure you leave details of your route. Heed local advice, listen to weather forecasts, and do not hesitate to change plan if conditions deteriorate.

Some of the walks in this book venture into remote country and others climb high summits, and these expeditions should only be undertaken in good summer conditions. In winter they could

well need the skills and experience of mountaineering rather than walking. In midwinter the hours of daylight are of course much curtailed, but given crisp, clear late-winter days many of the shorter expeditions would be perfectly feasible, if the guidelines given are adhered to. THINK is the only actual rule. Your life may depend on that. Seek to learn more about the Highlands and your part in them, and continue to develop your skills and broaden your experience.

Mountain Rescue

In case of emergency the standard procedure is to dial 999 and ask for the police who will assess and deal with the situation.

First, however, render first aid as required and make sure that the casualty is made warm and comfortable. The distress signal (six flashes/whistle-blasts, repeated at intervals of one minute) may bring help from other walkers in the area. Write down essential details: exact location (six-figure grid reference), time of accident, numbers involved, details of any injuries sustained, steps already taken; then despatch a messenger to phone the police.

If leaving the casualty alone, mark the site with an eye-catching object. Be patient; waiting for help can seem interminable.

 ## Useful Organisations

Association for the Protection of Rural Scotland
Gladstone's Land, 3rd floor,
483 Lawnmarket, Edinburgh EH1 2NT.
Tel. 0131 225 7012

Forestry Commission
Information Dept, 231 Corstorphine Road,
Edinburgh EH12 7AT.
Tel. 0131 334 0303

Historic Scotland
Longmore House, Salisbury Place,
Edinburgh EH9 1SH.
Tel. 0131 668 8600

Long Distance Walkers' Association
21 Upcroft, Windsor, Berkshire SL4 3NH.
Tel. 01753 866685

National Trust for Scotland
5 Charlotte Square, Edinburgh EH2 4DU.
Tel. 0131 226 5922

Ordnance Survey
Romsey Road, Southampton SO16 4GU.
Tel. 08456 05 05 05 (Lo-call)

Ramblers' Association (main office)
1–5 Wandsworth Road,
London SW8 2XX.
Tel. 0171 582 6878

Ramblers' Association (Scotland)
23 Crusader House, Haig Business Park,
Markinch, Fife KY7 6AQ.
Tel. 01592 611177

Royal Society for the Protection of Birds
Abernethy Forest Reserve, Forest Lodge,
Nethybridge, Inverness-shire PH25 3EF.
Tel. 01479 821409

Scottish Natural Heritage
Information and Library Services,
2 Anderson Place, Edinburgh EH6 5NP.
Tel. 0131 554 9797

Scottish Rights of Way Society Ltd
John Cotton Business Centre,
10/2 Sunnyside, Edinburgh EH7 5RA.
Tel. 0131 652 2937

Scottish Wildlife Trust
Cramond House, Kirk Cramond,
Cramond Glebe Rd., Edinburgh EH4 6NS.
Tel. 0131 312 7765

Scottish Youth Hostels Association
7 Glebe Crescent, Stirling FK8 2JA.
Tel. 01786 451181

Tourist Information:
Highlands of Scotland Tourist Board
Peffery House, Strathpeffer IV14 9HA.
Tel. 01997 421160
*Local tourist information offices (*not
open all year):*
*Ballachulish: 01855 811296
*Fort Augustus: 01320 366367
Fort William: 01397 703781
*Mallaig: 01687 462170
Oban: 01631 563122
*Spean Bridge: 01397 712576

Weather Forecasts
Mountaincall West
Tel. 0891 500441
Scotland seven-day forecast
Tel. 0891 112260
UK seven-day forecast
Tel. 0891 333123

 Ordnance Survey Maps of Fort William and Glen Coe

The walks described in this guide are covered by Ordnance Survey 1:50 000 scale (1$\frac{1}{4}$ inches to 1 mile or 2cm to 1km) Landranger maps 33, 34, 41, 42 and 50. These all-purpose maps are packed with information to help you explore the area. Viewpoints, picnic sites, places of interest and caravan and camping sites, are shown as well as public rights-of-way information such as footpaths and bridle-ways.

There is also an Outdoor Leisure Map 38, Ben Nevis and Glen Coe, at 1:25 000 scale (2$\frac{1}{2}$ inches to 1 mile or 4cm to 1km) which covers several walks.

Pathfinder maps, also at 1:25 000 scale, covering the area are:

249 (NM 89/99) Glen Dessarry
250 (NN 09/19) Loch Arkaig
251 (NN 29/39) Laggan, Highland
264 (NN 08/18) Glen Loy
265 (NN 28/38) Lower Glen Roy and
    Roybridge
292 (NN 46/56) Lower Loch Ericht
307 (NN 45/55) Loch Rannoch, West
332 (NN 03/13) Glen Kinglass

To get to the Fort William and Glen Coe area use the Ordnance Survey Great Britain Routeplanner, Travelmaster map number 1, at 1:625 000 (1 inch to 10 miles or 4cm to 25km) scale or Travelmaster maps 2, Northern Scotland, 3, Western Scotland and the Western Isles and 4, Southern Scotland and Northumberland, at 1:250 000 (1 inch to 4 miles or 1cm to 2.5km) scale.

Ordnance Survey maps and guides are available from most booksellers, stationers and newsagents.

Bibliography

Aitken, R. *The West Highland Way*, HMSO Revised edition 1990 (Guide and excellent background)

Ben Nevis and Glen Nevis, Wildlife and Geology, NCC, 1989 (Booklet)

Broster, D.K. *A Jacobite Trilogy* (comprising *The Flight of the Heron, The Gleam in the North, the Dark Mile*), Penguin, 1984 (Jacobite romantic novels)

Brown, H.M. *Climbing the Corbetts*, Gollancz, 1990 (Narrative of ascents)

—, *Hamish's Mountain Walk*, Paladin, 1980 (Non-stop over the Munros)

—, *Scotland Coast to Coast*, Patrick Stephens, 1990 (Includes several walks described here)

Buchan, J. *The Massacre of Glen Coe*, Lang Syne, 1991 (Classic account)

Cameron, A.D. *The Caledonian Canal*, T. Dalton, 1972 (The best history)

Crocket, K.V. *Ben Nevis*, SMC, 1986 (Story of the mountain)

Darling, F.F. & Boyd, J.H. *The Highlands and Islands*, Collins New Naturalist, 1964 (Superb ecological descriptions; still in print)

Drummond, P. *Scottish Hill and Mountain Names*, Scottish Mountaineering Trust, 1991

Great Glen, Wildlife and Landscape, NCCS, 1991 (Booklet)

Haldane, A.R.B. *The Drove Roads of Scotland*, EUP, 1991 (Fascinating account)

Heading for the Scottish Hills, MC of S/SLF, 1989 (Lists details of Highland estates)

Hendry, G. *Midges in Scotland*, AUP, 1989 (All you want to know!)

Hodgkiss, P. *The Central Highlands*, SMC, 1984 (General guide to area)

Howat, P. *The Lochaber Narrow Gauge Railway*, NGR Soc, 1980 (The aluminium-works line)

Kilgour, W.T. *Twenty Years on Ben Nevis*, Ernest Press, 1985 (Reprint of a Victorian life at summit observatory)

Langmuir, E. *Mountaincraft & Leadership*, SSC/SMLTB, 1984 (Standard work)

McGill, P. *Children of the Dead End*, 1914; reprinted Caliban Books, 1985 (Fictional account of building of the Blackwater dam)

Moran, M. *Scotland's Winter Mountains*, David & Charles, 1988 (Comprehensive practical information)

Munro, N. *The New Road*, many editions (Fiction; period of military roads)

Murray, W.H. *Scotland's Mountains*, SMC, 1987 (The natural and human story of the hills)

Place Names on Maps of Scotland and Wales, Ordnance Survey, 1981 (Useful booklet)

Prebble, J. *The Massacre of Glen Coe/The Highland Clearances/Culloden*, Penguin (many editions; a readable background to much of Highland history)

Scottish Rights of Way Society: *Rights of Way, A Guide to the Law in Scotland*, SRWS (Standard work)

Stott, L. *Waterfalls of Scotland*, AUP, 1987 (Comprehensive gazetteer)

Taylor, W. *The Military Roads in Scotland*, David & Charles, 1976 (Wade, Caulfeild, etc; recently reprinted)

Thomas, J. *The West Highland Railway*, David & Charles, 1965 (Evergreen story of the line, now in paperback)

Fort William and Ben Nevis

Index

Entries in *italic type* refer to illustrations